THE GOD OF THE GOSPELS

A Theological Workbook

Paul S. Minear

John Knox Press
ATLANTA

Unless otherwise indicated Scripture quotations are from the Revised Standard
Version of the Holy Bible, copyright, 1946, 1952, and © 1971, 1973 by the
Division of Christian Education, National Council of the Churches of Christ in
the U.S.A. and used by permission. Variations from the RSV text indicate
author's emendations.

Library of Congress Cataloging-in-Publication Data

Minear, Paul Sevier, 1906-
    The God of the Gospels.

    Includes index
    1. God—Biblical teaching. 2. Bible. N.T.—
Criticism, interpretation, etc. I. Title.
BS2398.M56   1988   231   88-45433
ISBN 0-8042-0545-0

© copyright John Knox Press 1988
10 9 8 7 6 5 4 3 2 1
Printed in the United States of America
John Knox Press
Atlanta, Georgia 30365

Contents

Dedication

To
Donald O. Hoffman
whose perceptive and persistent questioning
induced me to think on these things

Acknowledgments

Four friends have read and commented on these pages: Richard Davis, Hans W. Frei, Mary Knutsen, and Paul W. Meyer. I thank them warmly. In 1986, a class in the Graduate Seminary in Phillips University examined some of these texts with me. They, too, have my gratitude. Most of all, I have been helped by my wife's critical discernment and constant encouragement; that debt is beyond measure.

THE GOD
OF
THE GOSPELS

PROSPECT

> The proper way to determine what "God" signifies . . . is by examining how the word operates within a religion and thereby shapes reality and experience rather than by first establishing its propositional or experiential meaning and reinterpreting or reformulating its uses accordingly.
> —George A. Lindbeck, *The Nature of Doctrine*, (Philadelphia: Westminster Press, 1984, p. 114)

The goal in this study is to explore what the term *God* signifies as it is used in the Gospels. There can, of course, be little doubt about the importance of that term. The texts everywhere point to God as the magnetic pole of the world of thought. They assume that God is more important than everything else. God is the hidden source of thinking as well as its frequent object. Yet the references to God's role are normally oblique rather than direct. Because the narrators take it for granted that God hides behind and within human actions, each situation becomes an intriguing challenge to assess the role played by the Most High. To recapture that role requires penetrating the inner logic of the narratives. In telling their stories, the Evangelists place us alongside the participants in the original episodes, amazed or baffled by the assumption that the Eternal is present in that bit of temporal process. Every story puts us under a subtle pressure to perceive that presence. The narrator is fully aware of God's presence, and that awareness permeates the ways in which the story is told. But the God-logic (sometimes called theology) pervades the infrastructures of thinking rather than the surfaces of verbal expression. So we must rely on our own active intelligence to bring those infrastructures to the surface.

The central part of this book is labeled a theological workbook. Here the goal is to survey the range of evidence supplied by the Synoptic Gospels so that you may formulate your own theological conclusions. Some ninety texts are examined, one after the other, in the effort to penetrate the patterns of thinking that lie behind the patterns of speaking. The language of these texts at first seems quite simple and clear; this appearance, however, is very deceptive. The language is actually quite distinctive and difficult to follow. Accordingly, one goal of the workbook is to make the biblical language more accessible. Any language, to be sure, consists, not of isolated words, each of which can be defined by itself, but of complex and subtle paragraphs, reflecting not only the thought-patterns of particular authors, but the rich cultural traditions that lie behind them. In the Gospels, the term *God* does not represent a single concept in isolation, but an entire constellation of perceptions and attitudes. We will never comprehend this constellation apart from tracing the thought-pattern as a whole, the logic that links the insights of specific individuals such as Jesus to the cumulative experience of a community such as the early church.

This fact makes a choice of procedures both difficult and strategic. I have chosen to filter out all the texts in the Synoptic Gospels in which significant convictions about God are either expressed or implied. The texts are divided into four groups, according to the people involved: Jesus' conversations with his disciples; his conversations with his adversaries; his words to an unseen world, which included both Satan and God; and the Evangelists' reports of other strategic conversations. The justification for this division should become apparent in due course.

During this study, you will become historians to the degree that your objective is to recover the original thought-patterns in the texts that speak of God. This purpose requires that each text be placed in its own literary setting and in its ostensible historical occasion. Because the thinking expressed in a text often reflects the time, the place, and the people involved, you should study the literary unit as a whole and visualize the human situation as described.

You will also become theologians to the degree that you ponder the convictions about God that are explicit or clearly implicit in a text. Try to place each of these convictions within the pattern of attitudes indigenous to the text as a whole, attitudes without which the explicit convictions would make little sense. Take time to reflect on the implications to be drawn from those convictions of the Evangelists. This reflection will not be easy; indeed, it may be quite exhausting. It is not accidental that this study is called a workbook.

To become theologians, however, you need not try to arrive at a set of formal doctrines about the Deity. The Gospels themselves discourage such a goal. Each text points beyond itself to a mysterious fabric of personal and communal relations to God that can best be dealt with by using stories, short and long, and by correlating daily experience with multiple metaphors that point to God's active presence as creator, judge, father, and revealer of the secrets of human hearts.

And now, a word to my colleagues in the guild of biblical scholars. To focus on the God of the Gospels will lead us down paths rarely traveled in current historical studies. Scholars have not been greatly concerned about dealing with the Gospel witnesses to God's activity. Because this is true, I believe that historical study should do greater justice to the theological convictions of the Evangelists than has recently been done. Such justice is, in fact, a central intention of this workbook. In this respect, I applaud the comment of my colleague Brevard S. Childs:

> The basic function of the canonical writings . . . . was not to instruct the reader on the ideology of an author, but to bear witness to its subject matter, the Gospel. The individuality of the human author is subordinated to the theological significance of the life, death, and resurrection of Jesus Christ. From a canonical perspective, the primary function of the Gospels is theocentric, not anthropocentric.
> *The New Testament as Canon: An Introduction*
> (Philadelphia: Fortress Press, 1985), p. 153

Before turning to the texts, scholars have a right to know of two decisions that have been made on technical problems. First of all, attention will be focused on the Gospels in their completed form, not on the figure of Jesus or on the pre-Gospel traditions. Each document was written for believers who were aware of the story of Jesus as a whole; it was told by a Christian who was looking back at earlier events from the time when the Gospels were being written. Each Gospel represents the effort of an early Christian leader to fulfill his vocation within his own church. In giving priority to this later period, I do not imply any judgment, positive or negative, concerning the accuracy of the records about Jesus. The focus simply reflects the decision to concentrate on the perspectives of the Gospel authors as they addressed their own initial audiences.

In selecting and commenting on the texts, I have also decided to ignore differences in outlook among the first three Gospels, usually called the Synoptics. Scholars have spent long and fruitful hours in distinguishing among the theological positions and editorial methods of these three Evangelists. Often it is vital to recognize those distinctions. For our purposes, however, those differences seem negligible; rather, the study shows a notable homogeneity among the thought-patterns that refer to God. At times, to be sure, one author may describe a situation differently or draw different inferences from a given episode, but in the basic God-logic the outlook remains the same. Even where differences exist, the similarities need to be traced before those differences can be located and evaluated. The concern here is with detecting those similarities. The distance between the Synoptics and the Gospel of John is more substantial, although scholars may have been inclined to exaggerate those differences. However that may be, this workbook does not draw on evidence from the fourth Gospel except in marginal comments here and there.

A final word to potential readers. This book is organized to stimulate you to become your own theologians, resident in your own homes and churches. Accordingly, I have made little effort to draw up a set of doctrinal conclusions. You are, of course, free to do that, but the workbook is designed more to provoke thought than to establish conclusions. Each comment on a text is an invitation to you to agree or to disagree. You are urged to supplant each comment with a better one or to replace it with your own observation. It is far more desirable for you to grapple on your own with each text than to share my observations. Of course, it may be that you have no desire to become a theologian, (an unpopular label in many circles). In that case, you may prefer a less loaded word, such as archaeologist.

When archaeologists, in exploring an ancient tomb, encounter dusty artifacts—a bit of pottery, some coins, jewelry, perhaps— they use each artifact as part of a larger puzzle. They want to reconstruct some aspect of the communal life in which a tool or a dish was used. Each new find is added to earlier finds from the same place and period; together they throw light on the ancient scene. It is not too farfetched to treat each text in this workbook similarly, as belonging within an ancient world of thought, to be used in the recovery of ancient habits and patterns of thinking. Those patterns, in turn, make each text more intelligible than it would otherwise be. In this complex process of putting the puzzle together, a high degree of disciplined imagination is necessary, an imagination with which we make a greater effort to transport ourselves into that ancient world of thought rather than to exploit the text to serve current fashions in our own thought-world. For example, most of the texts about God in the Gospels were first used in the worship of the Christian churches. Their shape and their contours reflect that habitat. They point beyond themselves to prayers and hymns, to prophetic proclamations or probing meditations, used by congregations engaged in glorifying the Father of Jesus Christ, who is revered as the Father of every believer. When these liturgical and ethical affiliations are recognized, the logic of the God-talk becomes much more transparent.

No such study can be free from the risks that accompany all human talk about God. Talk tends to conceptualize and verbalize realities that cannot be reduced to concepts or words. It is all too easy to turn profound mystery into banality and to turn the freedom of the human spirit into bondage to pious clichés. Presumption is always near at hand; in speaking about the Divine, we often claim to know more than we actually do. Thoughts as well as speech can be blasphemous, a risk that is far greater for believers than for agnostics. Such dangers cannot be avoided in a study like this. Yet it may reduce those dangers if we concern ourselves not so much with the adequacy of our own attitudes as with the patterns of thought and the speech of the three Evangelists, whose work from the first has been trusted by the church to disclose the enduring significance of God's presence in the activity of Jesus of Nazareth, after as well as before his death.

Any book published today initiates a conversation between its modern author and its readers. In this book, however, a far more important conversation may emerge between you and the three ancient editors of the traditions about Jesus. Because most of you belong to one of three groups, let me make several suggestions that may help you learn to read the Gospels with greater penetration into the Evangelists' thinking about God.

The first group is made up of adult Christians who, as a part of their daily schedule, have set aside a period for meditation and reflection about things that matter most. For you, this workbook provides ample food for three months if each day you concentrate on a different text. Because the treatment of a text is confined to a single page, you can cover that page in as little as ten minutes, although to do it justice may take much longer. All you need is a copy of the Bible and time to think on the theme at hand. It would, of course, be well for you to develop the habit of linking each text to some favorite hymn (e.g., text 19) or to a short prayer. Then that song or prayer can accompany you throughout the day.

A second group who may find this book useful is composed of students who have registered for college courses in religion or seminary courses in Bible or theology. Even if this book is not used as a formal resource, it may stimulate you to listen to the texts in a more intimate way than is possible in doing classroom assignments. On the other hand, teachers may choose the book as a basis for the term's work. Having tried this in a seminary course, I can recommend it, albeit with some trepidation. Daily discussions might cover two texts each, so that some forty texts might be covered during a term. To supplement these discussions each student might be required each week to prepare a one-page analysis of some text not covered here (e.g., Heb. 1:1–3; Rev. 5). Because the subject is important in several academic disciplines, team teaching can be used to advantage—in colleges by the teachers in religion and literature, and in seminaries by the teachers in Bible, theology, and liturgics. The subject is one that should elicit vigorous participation by all.

Finally, I visualize use of the workbook by teachers and preachers in local parishes who wish stimulating assistance in coping with their weekly tasks. If you are a minister, you may want to plan a series of sermons on God. You may have a group of members who share with you the study of a text on which you will preach the following Sunday. In that case, you can select a text from the workbook and have copies of that page mimeographed as the basis for that study. As a teacher, you may have an adult class engaged in disciplined study of the central issues of faith. No issue is more central than this. For an experimental six-week series you might select six of the most disturbing and least familiar texts from Section 1 and make available mimeographed copies of those six pages. As teacher, you could introduce the series and ask members to accept responsibility for introducing successive group discussions. Should the first series prove profitable you could plan a later series based on six texts from Section 2 . . . and then from Sections 3 and 4.

The publisher has designed the format to make possible many different uses. This is intended to encourage maximum initiative and flexibility on the part of all readers. Whatever the form of study, it is important to focus attention on the subject that we so often shy away from, even in churches and schools: the God of the Gospels. The title is not *God in the Gospels*, but *The God of the Gospels*. There is a vast difference between those two. Whatever your use and whatever your group, may you enjoy the quest.

JESUS
AND
HIS DISCIPLES

JESUS
AND
HIS DISCIPLES

> Any theologian understands martyrdom,
> but only the martyr experiences the fire.
> —Robertson Davies, *The Manticore*,
> (New York: Viking Press, 1976, p. 101)

Gospel writers thought about God by telling stories about Jesus. In telling these stories they affirmed their faith that his authority had been given to him by God and that this authority was directly linked to authentic knowledge of God. Each story reflects this authority and this knowledge. From many separate reminiscences about Jesus a single story emerged, a single sequence composed of many episodes. But the stories rarely picture Jesus alone; almost always he is engaged in a dialogue with an individual or a group. The individuals or groups, in turn, are representative of more people than those immediately present. Listen to each story, then, not as a solo but as antiphonal music, in which the responses are essential to full understanding. Most frequently the conversation takes place between Jesus and his disciples. One of his first acts was to persuade them to join him; his last act was to complete their instruction. Between that first and that last act was a period devoted to their training.

He had special tasks for them. Each metaphor that was applied to his work was applied to theirs as well. Shepherd—they also were shepherds. King—they also would sit on thrones. Prophet—they were a small school of prophets. Teacher—they were being prepared for similar work. To this end they left occupations and homes in order to be with him and to travel from one town to another in Israel. Early on, he made it clear that their work would lead to martyrdom, a warning ominous enough to daunt even the strongest. His call and their response set them apart from others, even from the larger crowd of believers. Their willingness to join in his mission is convincing evidence that they accepted his authority as messenger from God, with knowledge of God's purposes for his people. Their dialogues with him reflect this basic understanding. The same dialogues, however, prove how difficult it was for them to comprehend fully what he had to say about God. In each dialogue both bewilderment and understanding are to be discerned. What Isaiah said about God could have been said by each Evangelist about Jesus: "My thoughts are not your thoughts." In the study at hand, forty-two texts provide ample evidence of the difficulties in comprehending Jesus' thoughts.

On first reading, the narratives seem to place readers at the same place and time where things were happening. In accomplishing this goal, the narrators have shown a high degree of artistic skill. But of course they were really addressing Christian readers a generation or two after the latest event told in the Gospels. By that time all perspectives had shifted. Retrospect enabled the Evangelists to view both Jesus and his disciples from a new vantage point. All attitudes toward Jesus had by then been filtered through memories of his execution and exaltation, through his continuing presence as a living Lord with worshipers who now thought of themselves as his slaves. Belief in him clearly meant obedience to him; such obedience in turn meant acceptance of his authority as conferred from God. That authority, in turn, meant that as living Lord, he could reveal a knowledge of God that was unavailable through any other source. As a result all the accounts of his conversations with the original disciples were read with a new degree of comprehension.

Attitudes toward the first disciples had also changed. In the period when the Gospels were written, the disciples had become the revered pioneers of faith. As apostles, prophets, and teachers, they had completed the work for which Jesus had called them. Many of them had been martyred in the line of duty; some, under threat of death, had defected. Jesus' predictions about their fate, with which all the Gospels are punctuated, had been fulfilled. Their places had been taken by successors whose work, though under changed conditions, aimed at the same basic goals. Their specialized tasks, whether exorcism, teaching, governing, or consoling, gave them a sense of kinship with the first disciples. They had special reasons for observing the perplexities that the stories attributed to their predecessors. For them the stories of Jesus became conversations between themselves and the Risen Lord. The words "Jesus said to his disciples . . ." came to mean "the Risen Lord says to us . . . ." In the analysis of the texts, keep in mind this double setting: the time of Jesus and the time of the Evangelists.

A comment now on the organization of these texts. I use seven headings for each. First is the *Text*, a quotation from one or more of the Gospels that includes an explicit reference to God. Attention is focused on this reference. Second is *Situation*, which identifies the literary unit that needs to be read as a whole as one looks for clues to the attitudes toward God embedded in the quoted text. Under this caption also is a very brief comment on the historical situation—the time, place, and people involved in the story. Try to visualize this situation as a whole before moving on to the gist of the study.

Third is a section labeled *Convictions*. Here you will find those attitudes toward God that seem to be clearly expressed or implied by the text. Although these comments take the form of prosaic assertions, a question mark might be placed after each assertion. Do you agree or disagree that this comment is justified by the text? Can you discover in the text other convictions about God, adding them to the list? Should some of the statements be deleted or rephrased in clearer language?

Fourth is a section called *Assumptions*. Many of these sentences are much more problematic, inasmuch as they represent efforts to bring to the surface some of the hidden presuppositions that lie beneath and behind the convictions that have been specified. These statements are speculative—examine each one. Should it be accepted, rejected, rephrased, supplemented? Do the statements help you to reconstruct the patterns of thinking within which the convictions belong—logically, psychologically, linguistically, theologically? Unless you use your own critical imaginations in this area, the study will be quite fruitless, as well as unexciting.

Fifth is a section called *Implications*. Here I have tried to suggest various inferences that might be drawn from the pattern of convictions and assumptions that has emerged as I reflected on the text. Here again each assertion should become a question: is this inference rightly to be drawn from the text? If so, may other inferences be drawn from this one? How far can we follow the chain of inferences in our reactions to the conversation? Are these the reactions that the first readers of the Gospels would have had as they heard the Gospels read from Sunday to Sunday? It is in this area that the workbook may contribute most effectively to making theologians of its users.

That will not happen, of course, unless there are negative as well as positive reactions to the various texts. In the sixth section I have indicated what some of these *Reactions* might be on the part of contemporary American Christians. I have tried to counter the soporific effects of familiarity, which so quickly breeds contempt for the Gospel narratives. I wish to counteract also the subtle assumption on the part of Christian readers that Christians must agree with Jesus' views of God, or at least must suppress their instinctive disagreements. My suggestions about reactions are likely to miss the mark for many of you. In that case, I hope that you will formulate your own reactions as honestly and fully as possible, substituting your own diary readings for this section of the workbook.

Finally, I have added for each lesson one reference to an author outside the Gospels whose writing furnishes a foil for thought. Some of these references offer helpful historical background by way of similarity or contrast. In others, a modern poet or novelist relates the biblical theme to a nonbiblical situation. In still others, an episode in a biographical reminiscence throws light on the God-logic of the Gospels. In a few of the works, postbiblical theologians speak about a given biblical theme. The function of these references varies: to provoke argument, to help you bridge the distance between biblical and modern worlds, to facilitate quiet meditation on central issues. Here, again, I urge you to note in the margins similar materials from your own library of fiction, poetry, and biography.

TEXTS

1   God Sends a Messenger

TEXT

Jesus: I must shout the good news of the kingdom of God to the other cities also; this is the purpose for which I was sent [i.e., by God]. (Luke 4:43)

SITUATION
Read the first text, seeking clues to views of God.

Luke 4:42–43; Mark 1:35–38
Jesus speaks to "the people" who follow him and who urge him to stay with them, but he denies their requests.

CONVICTIONS
Are these five attitudes basic to the text?

God is one who sends; "I was sent" = God sent me.
This sending is in line with God's purpose.
The purpose is to announce God's kingdom.
God directs the messengers to go from one city to others.
God chooses both specific messengers and specific audiences.

ASSUMPTIONS
Do these five things lie behind the convictions about God?

Jesus' purpose becomes identical with God's purpose: "I must."
This sense of vocation presupposes direct knowledge of God's will.
This knowledge emerges from the deep recesses of self-knowledge.
Jesus' message draws its authority from God's commission.
Those who accept that message accept the authority of God.

IMPLICATIONS
Can we safely draw these five inferences?

A person knows this God only by accepting God's purpose.
A person can know that purpose only by sharing in it.
God's kingdom links the succession of spokespersons and their converts, city after city.
When God calls individuals to accept the news, he sends them in turn to public places on similar missions.
Any god who does not call and send specific human messengers is not the God of Jesus.

REACTIONS
Do you have other explanations of the sense of being sent?

The sense of being sent may be only the projection of a person's inner desires, even megalomania.
It may give recipients a feeling of superiority over those not sent.
These supposed messengers have no objective evidence to support their claims that they have been sent.
To start to think of God as one-who-sends is very different from many other starting points.

BACKGROUND

An earlier messenger—Isaiah 6

2 God Keeps a Promise

TEXT

Jesus: It is written of John:
"Look! I [God] am sending my messenger [John]
　　　　before your [Jesus'] face;
he will go before you to prepare your way [the road
　　　　to the cross]." (Matt. 11:10)

SITUATION
*Read all three passages
for clues to views of God.*

Matthew 11:7–19; Luke 7:24–30; Malachi 3:1
Quoting Malachi, Jesus is relaying a message from God. Matthew thinks of the
　　work of John and of Jesus as linked together by God.

CONVICTIONS
*Subtract from or add others
to these four.*

God had given a promise through Malachi and fulfilled it in John.
God had taken both steps to prepare the way for Jesus.
God addressed these words to Jesus, who understood and accepted them.
God acted through a chain of prophets, each of whom is sent to prepare the way
　　for successors.

ASSUMPTIONS
*What kind of thought-patterns
do these assumptions form?*

Scripture is to be regarded as a help in understanding what is hidden in the
　　present situation.
The past is to be read in terms of a continuing chain of God's messengers.
The present moment is to be viewed both as fulfillment and as preparation for
　　God's future action.

IMPLICATIONS
*Subtract from or add others
to these four.*

Apart from accepting specific spokespersons, one has no access to knowledge of
　　this God.
Acceptance of Jesus brings with it an acceptance of John.
Acceptance of either requires prophetic vision: "Look!"
Acceptance of either requires an understanding of Jesus' way as a fulfillment of
　　God's long-standing plan.

REACTIONS
What reactions do you have?

How curious to cite ancient scripture as a key to the present!
How odd for the Creator of all things to rely on messengers such as these!
What a narrow view of the past to reduce it to a highway marked by such
　　prophets as these three!
Did Malachi really have John in mind, and did John have Jesus in mind? If not,
　　is this view of God still valid?

BACKGROUND

The appointment of another prophet—Jeremiah 1

3 How to Become God's Host or Hostess

TEXT
Whoever welcomes you, welcomes me;
whoever welcomes me, welcomes the one who sent me. (Matt. 10:40)

SITUATION
Matthew 10:37–42; Mark 9:37; Luke 9:48; 10:16; John 12:44–45;13:20
In sending disciples on a mission that involves martyrdom, Jesus speaks
concerning those who will provide homes for them.

CONVICTIONS
God is the one who sent Jesus.
To welcome the visible Jesus is to welcome this invisible sender.
In welcoming visible disciples, hosts welcome the invisible Jesus and the
invisible God.
God is present wherever any member of this endless chain finds hospitality.
God's presence in disciples of Jesus' day created a danger both for them and
for their host or hostess.

ASSUMPTIONS
The chain of senders/sent is assumed to be endless.
However long the chain of human travelers, Jesus remains the essential link
to the Divine Sender.
To become God's host or hostess is highly desirable and equally dangerous,
for such hospitality invites persecution.

IMPLICATIONS
Hospitality to those sent is an essential road to knowledge of the Sender.
The context shows that to welcome Jesus is to welcome the cross.
It also shows that this principle of hospitality is universally applicable.
The principle holds true regardless of whether the host or hostess entertains
Jesus, prophets, the righteous, or even one of "these little ones."

REACTIONS
It is easy to transfer authority from a human sender to a human messenger but
very difficult to trace the authority of a human messenger back to the
Divine Sender.
It becomes doubly difficult when the messenger comes with a sword (Matt.
10:34–39) and when hospitality brings loss of life "for my sake and the
Gospel's."
To make loss of life the Divine Will seem to cancel out the picture of God as
a loving Father.
In principle one may think of a guest as God's *alter ego*, but in practice one
can seldom do that.

AID TO THOUGHT
Cf. G. B. Caird, *The Language and Imagery of the Bible* (Philadelphia:
Westminster Press, 1980), pp. 20–25.

4 A Son Knows Who His Father Is

TEXT Jesus: All things have been handed over to me by my Father,
and no one knows who the Son is except the Father,
or who the Father is except the Son,
and anyone to whom the Son chooses to reveal him. (Luke 10:22)

SITUATION Luke 10:17–24: Jesus responds to the success of seventy prophets.
Matthew 11:25–30: Jesus responds to the cities' refusal to repent.

CONVICTIONS Only this Son knows who this Father is, knows God as Father.
Only this Son can decide to share his knowledge of God.
Such sharing brings others into this family of Father and Son.
As Father, God chooses to share "all things" (e.g. authority) with the Son, and
    through him, with the family.

ASSUMPTIONS Jesus' thought requires the use of a twin metaphor—Father/Son.
Knowledge of either requires a revelation that is strictly limited.
Such knowledge is linked to a sharing in the Holy Spirit and in joy (Luke).
This exclusive gift explains the fall of Satan and the disciples' power over
    demons.
It also explains Jesus' rejection by the cities (Matt.11:20 f.).

IMPLICATIONS Those who think of God as the Father of all people are thinking of a different
    deity.
The knowledge of this Father/Son is implicitly equivalent to salvation.
Jesus denies this knowledge to the wise and limits it to babes.
In post-Easter worship this text could have been used as an invocation, a cry of
    defiance, a word of assurance, a promise to accompany baptism or eucharist.
Matthew makes this call to worship ("Come to me") a call to discipleship.

REACTIONS The saying fuses many offensive ideas. It asserts a unique knowledge of God
    and makes this knowledge exclusive. Such exclusiveness seems to be
    arbitrary, expressing the arrogance of a small in-group. It encourages self-
    deception, with humility masking pride and naïveté gloating over wisdom.
    The argument is circular. There is no way to test the truth of claims made
    for the Father or the Son.

ON THE USE OF Cf. Caird, *Language and Imagery of the Bible*, pp. 49–53.
GOD LANGUAGE

5   A Father Shows Who His Son Is

TEXT

Jesus: Who do you say I am?
Peter: The Messiah, the Son of the Living God.
Jesus: Blessed are you . . . for human wisdom has not revealed this to you, but my Father who is in heaven.
Jesus: Be gone, Satan. You are an offense to me. (Matt. 16:15–17, 23)

SITUATION

Matthew 16:13–23; Mark 8:27–33; Luke 9:18–22
At Caesarea Philippi, a turning point in the mission of Jesus.

CONVICTIONS

God is living; aliveness is an essential attribute of Father and Son.
The living God reveals what is hidden from human insight and wisdom.
Father and Son are metaphors pointing to a shared heavenly life.
What God revealed to Peter was hidden from others.

ASSUMPTIONS

God and Satan are ultimate rivals for Peter's mind and heart.
A person can receive knowledge of God only when God so chooses.
Satan finds it easy to abort such knowledge, even among the chief disciples.
The unity of Father and Son is embodied in the Son's suffering (Matt. 16:21).
That suffering explains why human wisdom cannot see the unity.

IMPLICATIONS

Both God and Satan can speak through Peter's own words. Peter does not know who is saying what, but Jesus knows.
God's revelation and Peter's confession establish a foundation for the church.
By implication, Peter's offense is also related to the church's foundation.
The text implies a linkage between Peter's offense and the blindness of the other disciples and of Jesus' adversaries.
The story as a whole (Matt. 16:13–23) implies that it was through Jesus' death that God finally showed them the identity of the Son.

REACTIONS

All the offensive elements in text 4 recur here. The story makes it clear that the Father/Son image is inseparable from the image of the Crucified Messiah. If the latter is either unintelligible or unacceptable, the former image must be rejected. That rejection would mean that in his rebuke of Jesus, Peter was speaking for modern readers as well as for ancient disciples and adversaries.

SATAN OR GOD?

Cf. Søren Kierkegaard, *The Gospel of Suffering and The Lilies of the Field*, trans. David F. Swenson and Lillian Marvin Swenson (Minneapolis: Augsburg Press, 1948), pp. 21–24.

6 God Gets a Family

TEXT   Jesus: Who is my mother? Who are my brothers? [Pointing to his disciples]
Look! Here are my mother and my brothers! Whoever does the will of my
Father in heaven is my brother and sister and mother. (Matt. 12:48–50)

SITUATION   Matthew 12:46–50; Mark 3:31–35; Luke 8:19–21; Hebrews 2:13; John 15:14
Present: Jesus, his disciples, one family, another family

CONVICTIONS   God is the Father of Jesus; Jesus is God's Son.
It is the Father's will, through Jesus, to create a new family.
Men and women become its members when they do the Father's will.
As bearer of this revelation, Jesus stands between this Father and this family:
    "*my* Father . . . *my* mother."
Through Jesus, God separates this new family from the old.

ASSUMPTIONS   Membership in God's family is the highest good.
Knowledge of God's will must precede birth into this family.
Jesus has such knowledge and wants to share it.
The meaning of all family terms (e.g., *sister*) is transformed.
Terms that have been sex-specific (male vs. female) now become obedience-
    specific (obedient vs. disobedient).

IMPLICATIONS   In an act of obedience three wills become one: God's, Jesus', the disciple's.
Jesus' *gesture* in claiming the new family is as important as his words.
Only one family can be God's; only Jesus can disclose its members.
Knowledge of the Father and the Son conveys knowledge of the boundaries of
    this family.

REACTIONS   The text forbids us to think of God as the Father of all human beings.
It also forbids God's children to give priority to the old families.
Thus all earthly family ties are devalued. How, then, are Jesus' demands any
    less obnoxious than those of many modern cults? And does the preference
    given to "Christians" undercut the dignity of all "non-Christians" as
    creatures of God?

GOD THE FATHER: Sallie McFague, *Metaphorical Theology: Models of God in Religious Language*
MODEL OR IDOL?   (Philadelphia: Fortress Press, 1982), pp. 145–64.

7   The Word Becomes a Womb

TEXT

A woman: Blessed is the womb that bore you and the breasts that nursed you.
Jesus: No, blessed are those who hear the word of God and obey it.

(Luke 11:27–28)

SITUATION

Luke 11:27–28; 1 Peter 1:23–25
Jesus has begun his journey to Jerusalem, to be rejected.
Surrounded by hostile bystanders, this woman admirer bestows this blessing
    on Jesus' mother.

CONTRASTS

Between the woman's blessing and Jesus' blessing
The blessing on Jesus' mother versus the blessing on obedient disciples
A babe born without choice to the mother versus disciples who hear and obey
    God by their own choice

COMPARISONS

God's speaking his word equals a mother's womb
Continued obedience to his word equals a mother's breasts
A baby's dependence on mother equals disciples' dependence on God's word

ASSUMPTIONS

There are two very different kinds of birth and two kinds of nourishment after
    birth.
When God speaks his word, some hear; others do not.
Of those who hear, some obey; others do not.
Those who obey are born and nourished through God's word.
God blesses them, and Jesus joins in that blessing.
That obedience and that blessing give a higher status to recipients than that
    given to Jesus' own mother.

IMPLICATIONS

Luke 11:29–32 defines this obedience as repentance.
Admiration for Jesus or veneration for his mother diverts attention from such
    repentance.
God has given Jesus a role similar to the roles of Solomon and Jonah (vss.
    29–32).
The text forces readers to redefine such basic family terms as mother and son.

REACTIONS

Can a church adopt contrary ideas of blessedness and still claim to accept
    Jesus as messenger from the Father?
Can a church obey this text as a Word of God and still share in the veneration
    of Mary?
Does every modern celebration of Christmas betray a misunderstanding of
    this text?

BORN OF THE WORD

John 1:1–18

8 Here and There

TEXT Everyone who acknowledges me before others
    I will also acknowledge before my Father in heaven;
everyone who denies me before others
    I will also deny before my Father in heaven. (Matt. 10:32–33)

SITUATION Matthew 10:28–39; Luke 12:4–9
Jesus predicts for his disciples trials before synagogues, councils, and governors.
    Having promised to follow him, they will be compelled either to confess or
    to deny him.

CORRELATIONS Their confession before others—his confession before God
Their word on earth—his word in heaven
Their word about him—his word about them
The present trial—the final judgment
Jesus' revealing of the Father to sons—his revealing of the sons to the Father

ASSUMPTIONS Jesus' action in his trial gives him authority to reveal God's action in their trials.
Their action when on trial will trigger both his action and his Father's.
Jesus' word discloses a verdict that would be hidden from those in the
    courtroom.
All legal terms now carry new meanings (e.g., innocent, guilty).

IMPLICATIONS Jesus and God are most present in the courtroom when least visible.
Because of Jesus' trial, all legal language becomes theological.
Trials force disciples to see new meanings in many words, such as
    truth/falsehood, weakness/power, death/life.
Language about God's final judgment becomes the logic of faithfulness under
    fire.

REACTIONS Because disciples face no such risks today, the teaching has become obsolete.
It is also obsolete because the image of Christ as an attorney in God's final
    judgment has lost credibility.
Thus all five correlations have ceased to operate in modern minds.

A MODERN TRIAL Hanns Lilje, *The Valley of the Shadow*, trans. Olive Wyon (Philadelphia:
Fortress Press, 1966), pp. 66–79.

9   Attorney for the Defense

TEXT

Jesus: You will be dragged before governors and kings for my sake, to bear testimony before them and the Gentiles. When they hand you over, do not be anxious how you are to speak . . . ; for it is not you who speak but the Spirit of your Father speaking through you. (Matt. 10:18–20)

SITUATION

Matthew 10:16–25; Luke 21:12–19; Mark 13:9–13
The coming trials of the disciples who confess faith in Christ

CONVICTIONS

When on trial, if they confess their "guilt," God's Spirit will be speaking through them.
Their testimony to their enemies will be God's speech to those enemies, whether Jews or Gentiles, religious or secular rulers.
Their human words will then become inseparable from God's word through the Spirit, opening up the possibility of repentance and faith for those enemies.

EXPECTATIONS

The testimony of the Spirit will prove their sonship to the Father.
Father and sons will then share the same goal: a message to the persecutors.
This very testimony is the reason that Jesus sent these lambs into the midst of wolves (Matt. 10:16).

IMPLICATIONS

The trial situation plus their courage enables one word, yes, to represent the speech of disciples/Christ/Spirit/God.
When the persecutors hear that one word, it becomes possible for them to hear all four voices in unison.
When disciples become aware of these other speakers, they will utter that word without anxiety.
The issue in all these trials is whether the inaudible word of God will be heard through the audible yes of defendants.

REACTIONS

If this text identifies the place where God speaks, where is such a place to be found today?
If there is no such place, how can God be known as the Father of sons like these?
Must the cross be made contemporary in other crosses before God's Spirit can convey the same fearlessness and honesty?

A PRISONER OF CHRIST SPEAKS

Philippians 1:27—2:13

10   This Judge Sentences to Hell

TEXT

Jesus: I tell you, my friends,
      Do not fear those who kill the body
          and after that can do nothing more.
      But I will warn you whom to fear,
          Fear him who, after he has killed,
              has power to cast into hell. (Luke 12:4–5)

SITUATION

Luke 12:4–7; Matthew 10:26–31

After Calvary, the disciples were tempted to defect in order to avoid capital punishment. For them, three choices collapsed into one: to keep silent or to speak boldly, to confess or to deny discipleship, to fear adversaries or to fear God.

CONVICTIONS

Only God has final jurisdiction over soul and body (Matt. 10:28).

Only God can sentence a person to hell.

Such jurisdiction belongs to God as Creator and Father.

There are only two fears and two deaths; a person cannot fear both deaths, but fears only one.

ASSUMPTIONS

The accused person's relationship to God is primal and final.

Jesus is wholly concerned with that person's final salvation.

This is why he stresses the correlation between salvation and every disciple's choices between two fears and between two deaths.

IMPLICATIONS

Two languages come into play in making these choices: two meanings of the terms *fear*, *death*, *soul*, *friend*, *power*.

Three things become fused: accepting the authority of Christ, the fear of God, and courage before persecutors.

The opposites also become fused: fear of persecutors, denial of Christ, loss of sonship, destruction in hell by the Father.

REACTIONS

In the absence of similar situations today, neither of the two fears and neither of the two deaths is a true option for disciples.

Does this preclude a full understanding of the God of Jesus?

Does it preclude also an understanding of God's love?

OUT OF THE DEPTHS

Roland dePury, *Journal from My Cell*, trans. Barrows Mussey (New York: Harper & Bros., 1946), pp. 3–10.

11   A Sparrow's Guardian

TEXT

Jesus: Are not two sparrows sold for a penny? Yet not one of them will fall to the ground without your Father. Even the hairs of your head are all numbered. So don't be afraid; you are more valuable than many sparrows. (Matt. 10:29–31)

SITUATION

Matthew 10:29–31; Luke 12:6–7
In preparing the disciples to face martyrdom, Jesus moves from a comparison of deaths to a contrast of values.

CONVICTIONS

Their Father is to be found wherever a hair is lost or a sparrow dies.
Even though as disciples they are no more immune to death than a sparrow is, their Father will be present in their dying.
It is God's presence and care that counts, not the length of life.
The fear of God produces fearlessness before enemies.

ASSUMPTIONS

For his comparison, Jesus chose the cheapest and most transitory things—a sparrow, not a lion—a hair, not a building.
The dying of martyrs can be equally insignificant and unnoticed.
God's presence in the death of sparrows underscores the vast difference between his scales of importance and those of any society on earth.

IMPLICATIONS

To think of God as present in a sparrow's fall is to begin theology at a different place and to move in a different direction than is true of the theologies favored by governors and kings.
God refuses to measure events in economic terms or in terms of wars and earthquakes.
Children of this Father must share his judgment concerning which lives are valuable in his sight.
The death of Jesus gives an awesome weight to this text.

QUESTIONS

What would happen if Christian newspapers and journalists measured newsworthy events by these criteria?
How ridiculous to use sparrows as measures of value and importance!
Does this teaching enhance or destroy the sense of human dignity?
If one had to join the company of falling sparrows to qualify for membership in God's family, who would want to do so?

AID TO THOUGHT

Fyodor Dostoevsky, *The Brothers Karamazov*, book 6, sec. 3 (g) (many editions available).

12   Satan Falls

TEXT   Returning from their work, the seventy shouted with joy: Lord, in your name even the demons obey our commands.
Jesus: I saw Satan fall like lightning from heaven. (Luke 10:17–18)

SITUATION   Luke 10:1–18
Jesus is bound for Jerusalem; the disciples are returning from their first mission. The text is also applicable to the post-resurrection work of the apostles.

CONVICTIONS   God had ejected Satan from heaven; Jesus had seen him fall.
God had thus given Jesus a share in the power over Satan.
Jesus' name had enabled the disciples to share this power.

ASSUMPTIONS   Heaven is the source of all power, divine and demonic.
Every person's heart is a battleground betwen those invisible forces.
The issue at every moment is whether God or Satan will determine a person's choices.
Jesus knows that Satan has lost the heavenly battle, and he shares this knowledge with his disciples.
Their success has been made possible as an extension of God's victory over Satan.

IMPLICATIONS   To grasp God's power one must struggle with Satan's power (demons, serpents) and then trust in Jesus' name.
Repentance and faith mark the point of transfer from the realm of Satan to that of God.

REACTION   The distance between ancient and modern thought-worlds is nowhere greater than here: the ideas of conflict with the demonic world; the visualization of heaven, where this conflict begins and is resolved; the practice of exorcism. Modern Christians do not (cannot?) describe daily life in these terms.

A HEAVENLY DRAMA   Archibald MacLeish, *J.B.* (Boston: Houghton Mifflin, 1956), pp. 3–24.

13 Walking on Snakes

TEXT Jesus: Look! I have given you authority to tread upon serpents and scorpions and over all the power of the enemy [Satan]. And nothing will be able to harm you. But do not rejoice in this, that the demons obey your commands. Rejoice only that your names are written in heaven [with God]. (Luke 10:19–20)

SITUATION Luke 10:19–20.
Jesus sends out seventy messengers as prophets, harvesters, exorcists. As lambs among wolves they receive authority over snakes.

CONVICTIONS The chain of authority passes from God through Jesus to these messengers in order to free others from demonic powers.
The messengers are called to share with Jesus the prophet's vision of the fall of Satan: "Look!"
Their joy should spring not from their mastery over evil spirits but from their presence with God, who is the source of their power and their security.

ASSUMPTIONS God alone retains final power over Satan and over the exorcists.
In this instance, power over evil is exercised by lambs sent into the midst of wolves.
The chain of authority is symbolized in the notion of names: the name of God, of Christ, of the seventy, of those who are healed.
That chain is also a chain of joy, the joy of knowing God as the victor over evil.

IMPLICATIONS There is a hidden link betwen "wolves" and "the power of the enemy."
Exorcists are warned not only against serpents but also against rejoicing for the wrong reasons.
Their joy should come not from their superiority over evil spirits but from their dependence on heaven.

REACTION It no longer makes sense to speak of Christians walking on serpents or of lambs sent among wolves. Because exorcism is no longer a common practice, this whole pattern of thought has lost its cogency. Such a God has ceased to be active.

A MINORITY OPINION C.S. Lewis, *The Screwtape Letters* (New York: Macmillan, 1943), letter 7.

14 Who Clothes the Grass?

TEXT   Jesus: Look at the birds: . . . your heavenly Father feeds them. . . .
Consider the field lilies. . . . If your Father so clothes the
grass of the field, will he not much more clothe you? . . .
Your heavenly Father knows that you need them all. (Matt. 6:26–32)

SITUATION   Matthew 6:25–34; Luke 12:22–31; Matthew 7:7–11; Luke 11:9–13
Because of the Father's love and knowledge, Jesus forbids the disciples to be
   anxious about food and clothing, even though their work threatens the
   meeting of such daily needs.

CONVICTIONS   God feeds the birds and clothes the grass, vivid symbols of worthlessness,
   transience, weakness, vulnerability.
The Father knows the needs of disciples.
God's fatherhood is defined by this very knowledge and concern.
Their sonship is defined by their trust in him and their victory over anxiety.

ASSUMPTIONS   The text applied with special force to traveling apostles and prophets, who were
   dependent on receiving hospitality.
The choice of metaphors (grass, birds) is a mark of the Father's total
   responsibility and the sons' total dependence.
For them to be anxious about daily food would mean the worship of another
   God—mammon.
After Golgotha this teaching gained force through memories of Jesus' trust and
   the Father's knowledge.

IMPLICATIONS   The disciples' anxiety about food formed a point in their lives where they were
   highly vulnerable to Satan's deceptions.
The text rejects all measurements of their lives in terms of length (how long did
   the daylilies survive?).
The boundaries of God's family are set by the real presence of God's care and of
   human trust.
The text rejects any measurement of God's care according to the needs of races,
   classes, nations, civilizations.

REACTION   To be human is to be concerned about survival, about tomorrow, about
   insurance, (birds and grass are subhuman!). This Father seems to demand
   behavior that is quite inhuman. Does any father merit the name if he
   provides no more security than this?

REFLECTION   Søren Kierkegaard, *Christian Discourses and the Lilies of the Field and the
Birds of the Air and Three Discourses at the Communion on Fridays*, trans.
Walter Lowrie (1939; reprint, Princeton: Princeton University Press, 1971), ch. 2
of *Lilies of the Field*.

15 Beware of Praying

TEXT

Jesus: In praying, do not heap up empty phrases as the Gentiles do; for they think that they will be heard for their many words. Do not be like them, for your Father knows what you need before you ask him. (Matt. 6:7–8)

SITUATION

Matthew 6:7–8
Jesus instructs his disciples, as future leaders in liturgy, on the kind of praying appropriate to the children of this Father.

CONVICTIONS

God is your Father (the plural your indicates a family).
His knowledge of his family is intimate and complete.
Praying does not add to his knowledge, increase his care, or deceive him about his children.
God's fatherhood does not extend to the praying of Gentiles or hypocrites.

ASSUMPTIONS

The text assumes that Jesus has authoritative knowledge both of the Heavenly Father and his human children.
The Father is closer to the children and knows them better than they know themselves.
Prayer consists of much more than petitions, more than telling God what he already knows.
Trust in the Father results in maximum simplicity and brevity in praying.

IMPLICATIONS

Simplicity and trust go together, as do verbosity and self-deception.
Children pray to the Father because of his prior knowledge and care, not because of his ignorance or indifference.
To listen to the Father becomes more important than to address petitions to him.
To use prayer as a way of exploiting the Father's help or of claiming special privilege proves that one is no longer his child.

REACTION

How many congregational prayers run afoul of this rule?
If obedience to this command is a mark of true children and true churches, where would one go to find them?
If they are not to be found, must we conclude that the Father is not to be found?

PRAYER IS DANGEROUS TO YOUR HEALTH

Georges Bernanos, *Star of Satan*, trans. Pamela Morris (New York: Howard Fertig, 1975), pp. 266–71.

16 Keeping a Secret from Yourself

TEXT When you give alms, do not let your left hand know what your right hand is doing, so that your alms may be in secret; and your Father who sees in secret will reward you. (Matt. 6:3–4)

SITUATION Matthew 6:1–4
Sermon on the Mount. The Father issues this command to his children, using as a foil the praying of the synagogue rulers. A sequel to the teaching on perfection (Matt. 5:48).

CONVICTIONS The Father sees perfectly what no one else can see.
The only alms he rewards are alms of which the giver is unconscious.
Receiving any reward from others excludes reward from God.
Only God can distinguish between altruism and egoism.

ASSUMPTIONS The inner conflict between altruism and egoism is a road that leads toward knowledge of the All-Seeing Father.
This conflict reaches maximum intensity in the performance of such basic religious duties as almsgiving.
To overcome self-deception in almsgiving requires reliance on the Father's knowledge, not on one's own.
All visible signs of righteousness are inherently deceptive, especially for leaders of religious communities.

IMPLICATIONS In Matthew's day the command would have been especially relevant because of extensive gifts to the church (Acts 2:44–45).
In that day, what seemed to be an attack on leaders of the synagogue was really a warning to leaders of the church.
In that situation the command became God's declaration of war on all pride in benevolent giving.
In the text God through Jesus and through his apostles carried that war into the worship of every congregation.
In all such worship the text reminded every believer of God's ability to see what is not seen by any person present.

REACTION Can any religious institution survive if it adopts this policy concerning benevolence? If not, does this establish hypocrisy as the law by which such institutions live?

THOUGHT-FUEL Dietrich Bonhoeffer, "Letters to a Friend," (letters dated July 16 and July 18, 1944), in *Letters and Papers from Prison*, 3rd ed., rev. and enl., trans. Reginald Fuller, ed. Eberhard Bethge (London: SCM Press, 1967; also Collier Books, 1972).

17　A Silent Conversation

TEXT　　When you pray, go into your room and shut the door and pray to your Father who is in secret; and your Father who sees in secret will reward you. (Matt. 6:6)

SITUATION　　Matthew 6:5–6
Same as Text 16

CONVICTIONS　　God, and only God, should be the one addressed in every prayer.
The secret presence of the Father is lost when the child who prays is conscious of the visible presence of others.
God will reward those who pray but only when God is more present to them than is anyone else.
All other prayers are not only hypocritical but futile.

ASSUMPTIONS　　Nothing is more central to religious life than prayer.
Prayer is inherently a secret dialogue between the Father and his children.
Prayer is an activity in which allegiance to the first commandment is tested.
Public praying in synagogue and church provides maximum testing of hypocrisy and self-centeredness.

IMPLICATIONS　　The paternal/filial relationship is either realized or destroyed in each child's prayer to the Father.
The greater the intimacy of that relationship, the greater the danger of hypocrisy.
Those who teach believers to pray accept a great responsibility for observing Jesus' command.

REACTIONS　　How can one obey this command without becoming conscious of one's own merit in doing so?
If God is the Father of only those who pray thus, who is the father of those leaders who are rewarded by public respect?
If this command were obeyed within the Christian church, what would be the result next Sunday morning?

A VISION OF PRAYER　　Charles Péguy, "A Vision of Prayer," in *Basic Verities: Prose and Poetry,* trans. Ann Green and Julien Green (1943; reprint New York: Books for Libraries Press, 1972), pp. 255–73.

18   A Mask of Joy

TEXT   When you fast, groom your hair and wash your face, so that your fasting may be seen not by others but by your Father, who is in secret. Your Father, who sees in secret, will reward you. (Matt. 6:17–18)

SITUATION   Matthew 6:16–18
Same as Text 16

CONVICTIONS   The God who is secretly present in these religious duties is also present in every other situation that his children face.
The Father who rewards children for these instances of total sincerity will reward them for all other sincere acts.
The Father is so intimately related to the hearts of his children that he sees the emergence of every desire for social approval, along with all other desires.
Sorrow before God may become the occasion for joy before others.

ASSUMPTIONS   The shape of desires is a sure clue to the god in whom one trusts, a clue much more dependable than public respect or personal self-confidence.
God's rewards are more to be desired than any other rewards.
But God's rewards are forfeited when a person confuses one's knowledge of God with one's own public image.

IMPLICATIONS   The text makes it impossible to tell when another person is or is not fasting.
The teaching on these three religious duties is designed to be extended to all other duties among children of this Father.
Therefore these children are enlisted in a lifelong struggle between social approval and God's approval.

REACTIONS   When one pretends joy in the midst of fasting, is this joy an example of hypocrisy or of sincerity?
What kinds of rewards are given in secret by the Father, who sees in secret? How do they compare with social approval?
By these standards, how does one measure the success or failure of a Christian congregation?
Can one become conscious of obeying these commands without illustrating disobedience by that very consciousness?

SELF-EXAMINATION   Psalm 139

Time-out

In almost every sport, players may call a time-out so that they can catch their breath or review the game plan with the coach. Perhaps we have reached such a moment now. If so, we should stop to ponder the difficulties we have encountered and to consider how they may best be surmounted.

One possible difficulty is the strange kind of mental exhaustion that often sets in when we try to respond to so many questions posed by so many texts. Each text raises its own set of questions for which there are no clear answers; and students must grapple with those questions on their own without relying on scholars to furnish pat answers. Like history itself, each text can be viewed as a box of puzzles to which the key has been lost. Efforts to find such a key can be hard work indeed.

A further source of difficulty lies in the very nature of thinking and speaking about God. Our modern world has not been helpful in this matter; it is adept in turning our thoughts and speech into other channels. We can talk without undue stress about autos or computers, but we quickly become tongue-tied when conversation turns to God. We have neither the ideas nor the words to cope with this topic and so are inclined to shy away from it. Theology becomes a foreign country whose language is used only by natives, and we have neither the desire nor the knack to master it.

That difficulty would not be so great if there were not a basic conflict between the biblical world and our own in thinking about God. The texts assume the potential presence and the activity of God in every situation; such an assumption is remote from the intellectual world inhabited by teachers and students today. Our world "is, first, essentially relativistic and, second, anti-supernatural, anti-numinous" (B.A. Mowat, "Seeing the Unseen," a mimeographed essay from the Society for Values in Higher Education, 1983, p. 3). Given that contrast, it is not strange that serious encounters with the biblical thought-world should leave us somewhat bewildered and fatigued.

Let me be a bit more specific about this, on the basis of the texts studied thus far. The God of the Gospels selects particular individuals and sends them to selected audiences with carefully chosen messages on which the future of those audiences depends. For many modern readers such an activity on the part of the Deity is all but incomprehensible. If such is the test of belief in this God, then we believe in quite a different deity. Again, the God of the Gospels is assumed to have a knowledge of human hearts and human needs that is superior to any human knowledge. God is present at the hidden source of every desire and thought; there God competes with Satan for the invisible determination of human behavior. We modern students have been immunized against such a view of our own lives or those of our peers. If such is the test of belief in this God, then we are either agnostics or unbelievers. Again, the God of the Gospels is one who calls into existence a community of the elect and gives to it a distinctive mission for all races and nations. Other societies are born and die within the span of universal history; this one alone draws its life from a realm that has no end, hidden with the Eternal. If acceptance of this attitude is essential to faith in the biblical God, many modern readers must ask to be excused. Finally, it is clear that the spokespersons for the God of the Gospels evoked among their own audiences both enormous enthusiasm and deadly hostility, as marked by the number of martyrs. It is not easy for people acclimated to an "anti-numinous world" to penetrate a world where such devotion and such enmity are elicited by such a God. These four contrasts are sufficient to illustrate the chasm existing between the God-logic of the Bible and that of modern readers.

Perhaps it is the effort of dealing with this chasm that fatigues us most. The texts themselves induce a subconscious awareness of the chasm and close off the easier roads of escape. When we study one or two texts in isolation from the others, we may succeed in forcing biblical thought into conformity with our own ideas of God. But the study of forty texts soon proves that success to be an illusion. Or we can set out, with the best of motives, to divest ourselves of the modern mind and its secularizing poisons in order to claim full entry into the God-talk of the Gospels. But sooner or later, this kind of levitation from one historical period to another proves illusory. The inner pressure to move in one direction or the other increases the mental strain and is ultimately self-defeating. The texts themselves do not deal kindly with either the desire to believe or the desire to defend the autonomy of the modern mind. They warn us against hasty acceptance and hasty rejection.

These difficulties may well cause you to halt your study. What can I say to encourage you to push forward? One thing is this: recognize some kinship with the audiences addressed by Jesus. Whether one speaks of his disciples or his enemies, it is clear that they had great difficulty in understanding him, especially in his thought and speech about his Father. Another thing is this: before agreement or disagreement is to be trusted, we should understand clearly the patterns of thinking that provoke either reaction. Most of us still fall short of that understanding. The remainder of this book is designed to cope with that deficiency. Moreover, it is a basic truth that we cannot understand thought about God until we understand the language in which that thought is clothed, and few of us can boast such an understanding. Hope for greater accuracy and adequacy in grasping that language impels us to continue listening to the Gospels. Progress in this matter demands that we concede to the Evangelists a genuine independence in thinking their own thoughts and in speaking their own minds, just as we claim such independence for ourselves. After we have fully recognized this mutual independence, we may in the end discover that they are in a position to speak about God with an authority that we cannot assert, even in our more presumptuous moments. With this observation, then, I return to the texts.

19   Eternal Life or Eternal Fire

TEXT

The King:
Come, you who are blessed by my Father, inherit the kingdom prepared for
     you from the foundation of the world. . . .
Depart from me, you who are cursed [by my Father], into the eternal fire
     prepared for the devil and his angels. (Matt. 25:34,41)

SITUATION

Matthew 25:31–46
A parable told by Jesus to his disciples and used by Matthew as a conclusion
     to all his teachings (26:1)

CONVICTIONS

God gives final rewards and punishments through the Son of man as king.
His verdict is a complete surprise both to sheep and to goats.
Neither group has been aware of Jesus' identity with the least of his
     followers, or of God's identity with the hungry, the naked, and the
     criminals.
Indifference to the needs of these groups guarantees that followers who are
     indifferent will share the fate of Satan and his angels.

ASSUMPTIONS

The parable reflects a church undergoing persecution, its members hungry
     and in prison.
In this situation, Jesus is more concerned for his disciples than for their
     adversaries.
Jesus' final judgment will do nothing more than disclose what is hidden
     within the present actions of the disciples.
Those actions and Jesus' judgment also reveal what has been hidden from the
     foundation of the world: to visit another disciple in prison is to be
     involved in both creation and final judgment.

IMPLICATIONS

A disciple's expectations of God's judgment are always mistaken.
The imprisonment and death of Jesus qualifies him to tell this parable as Son
     of Man and as King.
An inner logic of the parable corresponds to the inner logic of the Passion
     story, when disciples failed to identify themselves with this King.
One cannot believe in this King without recognizing his presence in "the
     least" of his followers.

REACTIONS

How can Jesus expect disciples to prepare for a judgment that will be based
     on merit and guilt of which they are unaware?
In view of this parable, can believers believe in a god of love without
     believing in a god of wrath?
Is God just in sending into eternal fire the disciples whose guilt is depicted in
     this story?

THE ALLEGORY EXTENDED

John Bunyan, *Pilgrim's Progress*, chs. 1—2.

20 An Unjust Sun

TEXT Jesus: Love your enemies and pray for your persecutors, so that you may become children of your Father in heaven; for he makes his sun rise on the evil and the good; he sends rain on the just and the unjust. (Matt. 5:44–45)

SITUATION Matthew 5:43–48
Anticipating their persecution as children of their Father, Jesus commands disciples to welcome injustices of many kinds.

CONVICTIONS "Your Father" controls the sun and the rain.
He sends sun and rain on the evil as well as the good, a mark of his love for the enemies and the persecutors.
God thus refuses to enforce justice between his children and their enemies.
To be like him, those children must pray for their persecutors.
Their prayers for their persecutors will be answered by their Father, who joins them in acceptance of injustice.

ASSUMPTIONS Believers have already received God's love while they were enemies.
Membership in God's family means suffering brutal and unjust treatment from enemies.
To be children of God is to surrender all claims for justice, vengeance, rights, dignity.
Praying for persecutors will give those enemies an opportunity to learn of God's love for them.

IMPLICATIONS Such praying shows how this Father/family relationship comes into being: "that you may become children. . . ."
God's treatment of evildoers establishes an inescapable rule for his family because it reveals how this family is created and destroyed.
The action of forgiving enemies brings invisible realities within the range of visibility; the present action of the family reflects God's past and future actions.

REACTIONS Most reactions to this text focus on the difficulties of human obedience. They should focus, instead, on the problematic picture of a God who chooses not to enforce a decent standard of justice. Other gods show partiality for the just. This God is as unjust as the sun and rain. And he requires his children to accept, and even to imitate, his unjust treatment of the good and the evil.

THE ALLEGORY EXTENDED Oliver Wendell Holmes, "Lord of All Being, Throned Afar" (hymn).

21   An Unforgiving God

TEXT

Jesus: If you forgive others when they are unjust to you,
your heavenly Father will forgive you;
If you do not forgive others who are unjust to you,
neither will your Father forgive your injustice to him.

(Matt. 6:14–15)

SITUATION

Matthew 6:14–15; Mark 11:25; Matthew 18:23–35
A central accent in the prayer Jesus taught his disciples

CONVICTIONS

By forgiving you, this Father has made you his children.
This act of mercy requires reflex action by you.
In the human act of forgiveness, two wills become one; the two acts, though
distinct, are interdependent.
The refusal to forgive guarantees the separation of those wills.

ASSUMPTIONS

The whole thought-structure rests upon faith in God as mercy in action.
Jesus claims full knowledge of God's mercy; by his ministry Jesus embodies
and verifies that knowledge.
All followers accept injustice as built into their vocation and as the point at
which God's forgiveness becomes actual.
As the acceptance of God's mercy to his children is a new birth, so their
refusal to forgive others is death for them.

IMPLICATIONS

The Lord's Prayer builds this logic into all genuine praying.
That prayer makes the refusal to forgive equivalent to being led into
temptation and delivered over to the Evil One (Matt. 6:13).
According to the related parable (Matt. 18:35), every creditor knows that his
or her debt to God is incomparably greater than any debt owed her or
him by others.
The God of mercy is near enough to the soul to discern the slightest deviation
from a forgiving heart.

REACTIONS

Can this law (and this God) ever become relevant to racial, economic, or
national conflicts?
Does faith in the God of mercy require surrendering faith in the God of justice?

THINKING ABOUT PRAYER

Jon Sobrino, *Christology at the Crossroads: A Latin American Approach,*
trans. John Drury (Maryknoll, N.Y.: Orbis Books 1984), pp. 158–70.

22 God Becomes a Father

TEXT

Jesus: Love your enemies,
Do good, and lend, expecting no return,
And your reward will be great,
And you will be sons of the Most High,
For he is kind to the ungrateful and the selfish.
Be merciful, even as your Father is merciful. (Luke 6:35–36)

SITUATION

Luke 6:35–36; Matthew 5:43–48
The basic covenant between Jesus and his disciples, based on this revelation of God's mercy

CONVICTIONS

The Father in heaven is merciful (In Matt., "perfect").
God's mercy is defined by treatment of the ungrateful and the selfish. God rejects punishment of the selfish, vengeance on the ungrateful, thus surrendering all claims to justice on the part of the disciples.
A child becomes a child of this parent through similar acts of kindness.

ASSUMPTIONS

Human society assumes the desirability of justice, equality, respect for human rights.
Normally, society expects its god to support such claims.
Jesus' teaching asserts a radical opposition between that expectation and the behavior of his Father.
He makes God's actions an absolute norm for the Father's children, forcing them to reject prevailing social norms and expectations.

IMPLICATIONS

This thought-structure conflicts with all systems of morality that are based on rights, dignity, equality, justice.
Thus it collides implicitly both with Jewish and with Gentile views of God and their appeals to divine sanctions.
The text rules out not only violence against God's enemies but also special protection for God's children.

QUESTIONS

If this command is the mark of fatherhood, where should one go to find the Father?
Does disobedience to this command establish disbelief in such a Father?
Does action that violates this command mark sonship to God's opponent, Satan?
Does such disobedience also define the term *world* as used by early Christians?

FOR REFLECTION

Karl Barth, *The Word of God and the Word of Man*, trans. Douglas Horton (New York: Harper & Row, 1957), ch. 1.

23　Twin Protests

TEXT

Jesus: It is God's will for the Son of man to suffer many things, to be rejected by the elders, the chief priests and the scribes, to be killed, and after three days to rise again.

Peter began to rebuke him. Turning and seeing the disciples, Jesus rebuked Peter: Leave me alone, Satan. Your thinking is based on human desires and not on what God wills. (Mark 8:31–33)

SITUATION

Mark 8:31–33; Matthew 16:21–28

A strategic episode in the story of Jesus and in his training of the disciples

CONVICTIONS

God has a mind: God thinks, plans, values, reasons, chooses.

God has chosen suffering, rejection, and death as essential to the vocation of his representatives—Jesus and his disciples.

Speaking for the disciples, Peter rejects this choice.

Satan uses Peter's rebuke to put Jesus on trial; Jesus uses the same rebuke to disclose the deception.

ASSUMPTIONS

God has chosen rejection by the religious leaders as an essential part of his plan.

Peter's answer places him and other disciples in the camp of those leaders, at least temporarily.

All opposing conceptions of Jesus' rejection and death are assumed to be traceable to Satan.

IMPLICATIONS

Trust in the God of Jesus requires recognition that alternative thinking is folly.

Disciples can testify to the truth of Jesus' insights only by action that embodies the same wisdom.

Such action is open to them whenever they face similar testing by Satan.

REACTION

In his rebuke of Jesus, Peter expressed human wisdom at its most convincing. During the intervening centuries, such a mentality remains as dominant as ever. Does history, then, vindicate the position of Jesus or that of Peter?

SUFFERING AS AN AID TO KNOWLEDGE

Léon Bloy, "Random Thoughts," in *Pilgrim of the Absolute*, trans. John Coleman and Harry Lorin Binsse (New York: Pantheon, 1947), pp. 346–51.

24 God Uses a Polygraph

TEXT   Jesus: Swear not . . .
                                   by heaven, for it is God's throne . . .
                                   by earth, for it is his footstool . . .
                                   by Jerusalem, for it is the great king's city. . .
                                   by your hair, for you cannot make one hair black or white.
                           Let what you say be simply yes or no. Anything more than this comes
                                   from the evil one.   (Matt. 5:32–38)

SITUATION   Matthew 5:33–37; 23:16–32; James 5:12; 2 Corinthians 1:17–20
                          One of the basic contrasts between Jesus' teaching and the law

CONVICTIONS   In all human speech, God is the source of truth and Satan the source of
                                  deception.
                          The choice between those two sources takes place when one decides whether or
                                  not to use an oath to support one's pledge.
                          The test of honesty lies in the source, not in the performance of oaths.
                          As the sole judge of honesty, God detects the slightest impulse to deceive.

ASSUMPTIONS   In swearing, to move from heaven to earth to hair does not diminish the gravity
                                  of an oath but enhances it, as God is nearest the heart of the person.
                          God's intimate knowledge of the heart makes all swearing futile, a denial of
                                  God's sovereignty over each yes and no.
                          No appeal to scriptural safeguards on swearing can secure honesty in speech.

IMPLICATIONS To appeal to God in an oath is to appeal to a god other than Jesus' God.
                          All swearing, not simply some oaths, is to be excluded on the basis of knowing
                                  how God is related to the heart.
                          By achieving purity in heart and speech, disciples can move far beyond the
                                  demands of the law as taught by the scribes.
                          The scribal rules are, in their effect, supportive of Satan's strategy.

REACTIONS   Difficulties in understanding this text spring from the unique aspects in Jesus'
                                  theological reasoning. Every church that has tried to forbid the use of oaths
                                  has failed, for this text lies far beyond the range of applicability by any
                                  human community. What, then, is its true function?

A TRUE STORY *The Journal of George Fox*, rev. ed., edited by John L. Nickalls (Cambridge:
                          Cambridge University Press, 1952), Ch. 1, pp. 474–88.

25   God Can be Seen

TEXT

Jesus: Blessed are the pure in heart, for they shall see God. (Matt. 5:8)

SITUATION

Matthew 5:1–10; Hebrews 12:14, 22–24

Jesus addressed this beatitude to the disciples for the sake of the crowds of followers. In this context "pure in heart" means single-minded, undivided in loyalty, sincere, uncorrupted.

CONVICTIONS

God is a reality that can be seen by one kind of seeing, by one kind of person who has the right kind of heart.

Such a vision is impossible to those with impure or divided hearts.

To see God is one definition of blessedness; along with the other definitions in Matthew 5, it is one of the marks of the poor in spirit.

God is closer to the pure heart than to the impure; this fact calls for revising many common ideas about God.

ASSUMPTIONS

Along with the other beatitudes, this text makes the vision of God a way of describing the highest goal.

It also explains the hiddenness, the invisibility, of God as due ultimately to human beings' inner blindness.

The other beatitudes indicate ways of moving toward purity of heart: meekness, peacemaking, mercy. . . .

Willingness to endure persecution is one measure of such purity (Matt. 5:10–12).

IMPLICATIONS

Jesus paradoxically offers here the highest reward to those who seek no reward; purity of heart and self-seeking are incompatible.

Because seeing God is one of the marks of prophecy, disciples who have access to this vision become potential prophets, i.e., revealers of this vision to others.

One of the qualifications of purity of vision is love of enemies and forgiveness of persecutors (cf. Matt. 5:11–12 with Acts 7:55–60).

QUESTIONS

Few Americans give high priority to a pure heart, to a vision of God, or to blessedness. The cultural situation has emptied this language of its original force. What changes in the culture or in the situation of the church might restore cogency to this language?

IS IT POSSIBLE?

Dag Hammarskjöld, *Markings*, trans. Leif Sjöberg and W.H. Auden (New York: Knopf, 1964), pp. 100–102.

26   A Holy Name

TEXT   Let your creation declare your holiness. (Matt. 6:9)

SITUATION   Matthew 6:9–12; Luke 11:2–4; John 12:27–33
The first petition in the prayer Jesus designed for disciples; the form shaped by
   use during the post-Golgotha period

CORRELATIONS   God has a name known only to his children; only they can declare his holiness.
Their name, saints (hagioi, "holy ones"), links them verbally to those who
   declare his holiness (hagiothetos).
This Father's holiness is the source of their holiness as a family and kingdom.
To hallow him is to ascribe to him alone the kingdom, the power, and the glory.

ASSUMPTIONS   God alone can fulfill such a petition.
By beginning and ending with him, the prayer expresses faith that all things
   begin and end with him.
He is an active God, who provides many things for his family: bread,
   forgiveness, rescue.
God's will, already realized in heaven, is now coming to earth through a family
   that declares his holiness.

IMPLICATIONS   The petition springs from the hearts of holy ones at prayer.
It is more at home in worship than in formal doctrine or moral exhortation (Rev.
   4—5).
The act of hallowing God unites the outer and inner zones of reality.
To declare God's holiness is the same as doing everything "to the glory of God"
   (1 Cor. 10:31).

REACTIONS   Because the prayer was specially designed for this one family, it does not
   properly belong to families who do not hallow the same name. And when it
   is used by Christian bodies who ignore its initial meanings and the
   safeguards for its use (Matt. 6:1–18), it convicts them of hypocrisy. In fact,
   its public use today almost always collides with those safeguards.

TRUTH IN FICTION   Petru Dumitriu, *Incognito*, trans. Norman Denny (New York: Macmillan,
   1964), pp. 452–54.

27   The Father Is a King and a Judge

TEXT

Jesus:
You are those who have continued with me in my trials.
As my Father has appointed a kingdom for me,
    so do I appoint a kingdom for you,
that you may eat and drink at my table in my kingdom
    and sit on thrones judging the twelve tribes of Israel. (Luke 22:28–30)

SITUATION

Luke 22:28–30; Matthew 19:28
The new covenant between Jesus and his disciples at the Last Supper; his final
    commission and his effort to prepare them for their trials after his death

CONVICTIONS

As "my Father," God controls all thrones and kingdoms.
As king, God has assigned his kingdom to Jesus.
Jesus has authority to appoint disciples to share in that kingdom.
To be a king is to function also as a judge of the twelve tribes.
Thus judging, ruling, and eating are metaphors describing the realm shared
    by God with Jesus and the disciples (cf. Luke 22:30).

EXPECTATIONS

The metaphor father intersects with the metaphors king and judge.
The sole condition for inclusion in this common realm is enduring Jesus'
    trials by enduring their own persecution.
After Jesus' death this promise became the pledge of the risen Lord, which
    was uttered at common meals.
Because the source of trials is Satan, a share in the kingdom means a share in
    Jesus' victory over Satan (Luke 22:31).

IMPLICATIONS

The reference to Satan helps to define the borders of the kingdom of Jesus
    and his disciples.
God is to be found wherever Jesus is and wherever disciples continue in his
    trials.
Like Peter, all disciples face a sifting by Satan; the whole teaching is a prayer
    that their faith may not fail (Luke 22:32).

REACTIONS

Those disciples never served as judges of the twelve tribes.
Few churches have ever claimed to fulfill that particular role.
Accordingly, it is quite impossible to locate those thrones, those kings, that
    kingdom. Does this force us to conclude that Jesus' Father did not
    appoint Jesus to the kingdom?

**THE REVOLT
AGAINST FATHERHOOD**

William Adolph Visser't Hooft, *The Fatherhood of God in an Age of
Emancipation* (1982; paperback reprint, Philadelphia: Westminster Press,
1983), pp. 95-100.

28 One Father Only

TEXT Jesus: Call no man your father on earth,
for you have one Father, who is in heaven. (Matt. 23:9)

SITUATION Matthew 23:1–12
Speaking to the disciples and to the crowd (leaders and laity in churches), Jesus requires of them behavior unlike that of scribes and Pharisees.

CONVICTIONS God is the Father, in heaven, of all believers.
God preempts that title and forbids its use for others.
As there is only one Father, he can have only one family.
Jesus prohibits the use of any titles that would foster or imply differences in status among his followers.

ASSUMPTIONS A community uses titles as a means of conferring honors, special privileges, and moral superiority.
One function of Christian teachers is to resist this procedure and to require equality among students and between teachers and students.
Followers have a duty to refuse to recognize the superiority of their leaders by the use of honorific titles.
God's kingdom differs from all other kingdoms in its embodiment of this truth.

IMPLICATIONS God has authorized Jesus to sit in Moses' seat, as do the scribes.
Teachers who sit there vindicate Moses' authority, not by claiming the privilege of office, but by enforcing this kind of humility.
For a Christian teacher to accept superiority over other Christians would be to deny God's fatherhood.
To be a member of this family is the highest conceivable status; brother is a term that includes both sexes.

REACTION Jesus based his demand for equality among his followers on his convictions about God. Because every church, with its ladders of offices, ignores Jesus' prohibition, no church can legitimately claim to be this family. Every negotiation on church union finds the problem of agreeing on ministerial orders virtually insoluble. Does this mean that in practice all our churches agree with the scribes and Pharisees against Jesus?

AN ACT OF OBEDIENCE *Journal of George Fox*, ch. 2 (pp. 22–39)

29 The Unseen Angel

TEXT

Jesus: Don't despise [or lead astray] one of these little ones. . . . Their angels in heaven always look on the face of the Father. [parable of the Hundred Sheep] So it is not the will of my [or your] Father . . . that one of these little ones should perish. (Matt. 18:10–14)

SITUATION

Matthew 18:10–14
Jesus prepares disciples for future work in church government (cf. Luke 15:3–7).

CONVICTIONS

By going one-on-one, this Father defies all statistical standards of importance (one vs. ninety-nine).
He prefers the least important sheep to the most important.
He searches for the lost sheep, finds it, and rejoices over its recovery.
He keeps open a hot line for appeal from the weakest believer.
He holds leaders accountable whenever they despise or mislead any follower.

ASSUMPTIONS

God's actions must determine human yardsticks for measuring the importance of individuals.
Jesus knows God well enough to know "what makes him happy" (Caird, *Language and Imagery of the Bible*).
The Father's policies must be carried out by leaders; he knows when they are ignored.
The humblest child has a defense attorney in heaven; the most respected leader may find a prosecuting attorney there.

IMPLICATIONS

The parable implicitly defines the extent of God's care, the adequacy of his knowledge, the range of his power.
The theology of church leaders is quietly conveyed by their care for the least and the lost.
God's rejection of numbers and status condemns all human tendencies to depend upon both.

REACTIONS

This text seems to justify the Nietzschean criticism that the Christian gospel gives priority to the weakest members of any society. Can any social institution survive if it enforces this rule, which Jesus made binding upon his followers?

THE PARABLE, FIRST EDITION

Ezekiel 34

30   God Ties and Unties

TEXT
Jesus: Truly I say to you [plural];
Whatever you bind on earth will be bound in heaven [by God],
Whatever you loose on earth will be loosed in heaven [by God].
    Again I say to you,
If two of you agree on earth about anything you ask,
it will be done for them by my Father in heaven. (Matt. 18:18–19)

SITUATION
Matthew 18:15–20
Jesus gives the leaders of the churches authority as judges.

CONVICTIONS
The Heavenly Father is a judge whose decision is final.
Jesus' assurance is authorized by God ("Truly I say to you").
God shares judging power with Jesus' disciples.
God also promises to support the disciplinary verdicts of those disciples.

ASSUMPTIONS
The metaphor of binding and loosing may refer to forgiveness of sin, to power to excommunicate, to power to free individuals from Satan and his demons or to all three.
Every sin against a believer is a sin against the church and against God.
It is because the gift of family is so miraculous that a sin against its members is so terrible.
The church is a realm of salvation where God's authority, both to bless and to curse, is manifest.
A refusal to listen to the church is an ultimate sin.

CONTRADICTIONS
An unresolved contradiction: seventy times seven acts of forgiveness versus exclusion of a believer before 490 forgivenesses
Another unresolved contradiction: the action by God and Christ through the apostles versus the prayers of any two members of the congregation
The text invites great confusion between heavenly reality and earthly politics, in which personal prejudices and in-group/out-group animosities operate.

QUESTIONS
How can one trust the Heavenly Father, who has given such final authority to such fallible judges?
Can the channel between heaven and earth be safely located in judicial actions like these?

THINKING IN MYTH
Northrop Frye, *The Great Code: The Bible and Literature* (1982; paperback reprint, New York: Harcourt Brace Jovanovich, 1983), pp. 71–77.

31   God Prefers Sinners

TEXT

The Pharisee in the temple: God, I thank you that I am not like other men.
The tax collector: God be merciful to me, a sinner.
Jesus: This man went down to his house justified, rather than the other.
Everyone who exalts himself will be humbled; whoever humbles himself will be exalted. (Luke 18:11, 13–14)

SITUATION

Luke 18:9–14
A parable spoken by Jesus on his final journey to Jerusalem, to followers
    who trusted in themselves and despised other followers.

CONVICTIONS

God's verdict reverses expectations previously held by Christians.
That verdict is visualized as being rendered in and through prayer.
The verdict can be described either as justification or as exaltation.
God prefers a contrite sinner to a grateful Pharisee.

ASSUMPTIONS

Jesus discerned both the hearts of worshipers and the responses of God.
Both prayers were sincere; they simply visualized different gods.
Justification or exaltation by God was assumed to be the supreme goal.
When the two men reached home, everything was different for one, but
    everything remained the same for the other.

IMPLICATIONS

The languages the two men used were the same, yet they carried different
    meanings.
Before God, any sense of being superior to others is a self-deception.
God knew the needs of both men before they entered the temple; the action of
    praying did not change their hearts.

REACTIONS

After praying, neither man was changed. What benefit, then, is justification?
The ultimate issue is not the difference between these two men, but the
    difference between their gods. Which god was on the side of which man?
Did one man's penitence cancel out his record of extortion and injustice (vs. 11)?

FOR MEDITATION

Augustine, *The Enchiridion*. chs. 30–33.

32   He Will Vindicate the Faithful . . . If Any

TEXT

Jesus: Will not God vindicate his elect, who cry to him day and night? Will he delay long over them? I tell you, he will vindicate them speedily. Nevertheless, when the Son of man comes, will he find faith on earth? (Luke 18:7–8)

SITUATION

Luke 18:1–8
The parable of the unrighteous judge ends with this point and this warning, in a conversation with disciples en route to the cross.

CONVICTIONS

God is a judge whose justice can be trusted by his elect.
He will vindicate them even more speedily than the human judge in the parable.
There is more reason to doubt the fidelity of the elect than to doubt God's vindication of them.

ASSUMPTIONS

The elect face only one issue: to be or not to be faithful.
Speaking with sure knowledge, Jesus is more confident of God's justice than of the disciples' faith.
Jesus tries to shift the attention of the elect from questions of when and where to questions about their own hearts: would they be as stubborn as the widow, as penitent as the tax collector (vs. 13), as confident as Jesus?

IMPLICATIONS

The coming of the Son of man may not be as desirable as the "elect" expect.
Their messianic impatience may prove their disobedience to the first commandment.
Like the unjust judge, God seems to dally with the cries of helpless widows among his people.
Unlike the judge, God's vindication of the elect comes speedily, though less visibly.

REACTION

Human history since the parable casts doubt on God's speed in vindicating the elect. Was Jesus right or wrong in his convictions about God? Or is it that speed and the vindication are matters that cannot be measured by any visible result in earthly history?

A POET'S VISION

Amos Niven Wilder, *Grace Confounding* (Philadelphia: Fortress Press, 1972), pp. 47–48.

33 God Controls the Calendar

TEXT
Jesus: There will be such tribulation. . . . If the Lord had not shortened the days, no human being would be saved; but for the sake of the elect, whom he chose, he shortened the days. (Mark 13:19–20)

SITUATION
Mark 13:14–20; Matthew 24:15–22
Jesus' preparation of disciples for dealing with false prophets within the church and with violent persecutors outside

CONVICTIONS
God created all things (Mark 13:19), and God continues to create.
God has control of the times and has shortened the period.
God has already done this for the sake of the persecuted elect.
But this shortening must not be used to feed apocalyptic excitements.
Rather, insight and endurance are required of God's people.

ASSUMPTIONS
God's choice of the elect is more dependable than their own calculations of the times.
God's choosing them supplies the ultimate brackets within which their vocation is set.
They must see their present as having been planned with their salvation in view.
Their confidence in God must be different from the frenetic impatience of false prophets and messiahs.

IMPLICATIONS
Memories of this teaching should discourage fears of catastrophe.
Disciples must distinguish between the signs and wonders of false prophets and the signs of God's control of the days.
Election is designed to produce endurance, not an accurate knowledge of the future.

REACTIONS
Since this promise was made, nineteen centuries have passed. How short a period is that?
Jesus' message here has been fully disproved by history. Can we continue to rely on it?
His predictions have caused endless confusion and many eccentric religious crusades. Isn't such confusion inevitable when any action of God is pegged to a particular date on a human calendar?

GOD IN HISTORY, HISTORY IN GOD
Richard Kroner, *How Do We Know God? An Introduction to the Philosophy of Religion* (New York: Harper & Bros., 1943), pp. 118–32.

34 The Father Sets All Schedules

TEXT   Jesus: This generation will not pass away before all these things take place. Heaven and earth will pass away, but my words will not pass away. But of that day or that hour no one knows, not even the angels in heaven, nor the Son, but only the Father. Take heed. (Mark 13:30–33)

SITUATION   Mark 13:30–37; Matthew 24:34–36; Luke 21:32–36; Acts 1:6–8
Jesus' final instructions to the disciples in Jerusalem immediately before his arrest and trial. He is warning against false prophets, who encourage either frantic excitement or apathetic unconcern.

CONVICTIONS   The Father controls the schedules and sets the times.
Those times are vocation-specific; i.e., the time is adapted to the mission.
God conceals knowledge of the future in order to test the alertness of the watchers assigned to the estate.
Jesus' words about God live longer than the duration of any generation.

ASSUMPTIONS   The expectations of true prophets should be very different from those of false prophets; such expectations of the end are a function of disciples' dependence on God and God's dependence on them.
The future as seen by God's children is shaped by these coordinates: the Father's call and commission, Jesus' words, the children's duties, their watchfulness for the time of accounting.
Attitudes toward the future should express a way of living according to those coordinates.
The hour of Jesus (Mark 15) becomes a parable of their hour; when that hour comes they will discover the validity of his words (13:31).

IMPLICATIONS   The children of this Father measure time, not in terms of centuries or of the rise and fall of nations, but in terms of a previous commissioning and a coming accounting.
This grammar of expectation makes every situation an ad hoc test of their reliability as stewards and witnesses.
Jesus' example in watching for his hour discourages both apathy and hysteria with regard to a final accounting.

REACTION   This sense of time did not survive the first century. It is entirely archaic today, and efforts to revive it are doomed.

THOUGHTS OF A NOVELIST   Morris West, *The Clowns of God* (New York: Bantam Books, 1982), pp. 67–71.

35 God Says, "Fool!"

TEXT

A rich man: I will say to my soul, Soul, you have ample goods laid up for many years; take your ease, eat, drink, be merry.
God: Fool! This night your soul is required of you. (Luke 12:19–20)

SITUATION

Luke 12:13–21
En route to Jerusalem, Jesus is speaking to the crowds of followers, with the disciples present. He draws a sharp contrast between "many years" and "this night," between everything and nothing, between two souls.

CONVICTIONS

God is the judge to whom every soul must give an accounting.
Night comes whenever God determines to hold such an accounting.
God interrupts a person's dialogue within the self and requires a dialogue with God.
God declares human wisdom to be folly and human measurements of security to be deceptive.

ASSUMPTIONS

As creator of the soul, God asks of every creature, "Toward whom are you rich?"
God's timing "this night" plays havoc with man's "many years."
Security concerning the human future is poverty toward God.
The moment of self-satisfaction is the moment for drastic judgment.

IMPLICATIONS

Children of this Father (vs. 32) must not appeal to Jesus to secure justice from other children (vss. 13–14).
Life in this new family excludes greed and security.
This family replaces the question "What belongs to me?" with the question "To whom do I belong?"

REACTION

Fool? By no means. By all human standards this man was very wise. Every current social institution and custom marks him as wise in gaining security against his future. It is Jesus whom communities today would call foolish, thus implicitly rejecting Jesus' view of God. Is this view of the soul, pictured in the parable as facing an accounting "this night," rightly construed?

SETTING THE TEXT TO MUSIC

Johannes Brahms, *A German Requiem*, movement 3

36 Attorney for the Prosecution

TEXT Jesus: What does it profit anyone to gain the whole world and forfeit his life? . . . For whoever is ashamed of me and of my words in this adulterous and sinful generation, of that person the Son of man will be ashamed when he comes in the glory of his Father with the holy angels. (Mark 8:36, 38)

SITUATION Mark 8:34–38; Matthew 16:24–28; Luke 9:23–27; Matthew 10:33; Luke 12:9
Jesus requires self-sacrifice both of the multitudes and his disciples; this is based on his confidence in the coming judgment by God.

CONVICTIONS The realm of glory shared by the Father, the angels, and the Son of man is a realm open only to those who lose their lives "for my sake and the gospel's."
God's glory is the antithesis of the shame before one's peers when one is placed on trial.
The suffering Messiah will be an attorney for the prosecution of those followers who try to save their lives when facing martyrdom.
The coming of God's kingdom is not defined by a prescribed date but by a disciple's tasting of death in the path of duty (Mark 9:1).

ASSUMPTIONS Every disciple must decide whether to be ashamed to acknowledge that he or she is a follower of Jesus or to be glorified by God.
God's future is thus hidden within the decision of a disciple, whether to forfeit life or to deny Christ.
The apocalyptic imagery links a martyr's inner struggles to God's final judgment and also links immediate profit to ultimate loss.

IMPLICATIONS Life and death are defined in new ways; these new definitions become essential to the language of discipleship.
New definitions of sin and adultery (Mark 8:38) are made to conform to the new definitions of life and death, shame and glory.
These shifts in vocabulary mark a shift in expectations concerning the when and where of final judgment by the Father.

QUESTION Since the text requires radically new definitions of such basic terms as life and death, shame and glory, the text has no cogency in a world that lives by the older definitions. In that saner world this teaching can only seem an insane glorification of kamikaze behavior. Can one defend Jesus' knowledge of God as true without accepting this understanding of God's demands?

ONE ANSWER Walker Percy, *The Second Coming* (New York: Farrar, Straus & Giroux, 1980), pp. 271–74.

37   The Greatest Miracle

TEXT

Jesus: It is easier for a camel to go through a needle's eye than for a rich man to enter the kingdom of heaven.
Disciples: Then who can be saved?
Jesus: With mortals it is impossible, but not with God; for all things are possible with God. (Mark 10:25–27)

SITUATION

Mark 10:23–31; Matthew 19:23–30; Luke 18:24–30; 1:37
En route to Jerusalem, Jesus disappoints a rich man and provokes this key question from the disciples.

CONVICTIONS

God alone keeps control over entrance into his kingdom, i.e., life.
God has given Jesus knowledge of the conditions for entrance, e.g., surrender of wealth.
God's power appears negatively in the rich man and positively in the disciples, who have surrendered everything to follow Jesus.
In disclosing the futility of wealth, the story discloses the power of God.

ASSUMPTIONS

The rich man symbolizes power, security, self-reliance, and despair.
Salvation, life with God, is the miracle of giving up all and gaining all.
This miracle of God's power takes place in the hearts of those Jesus calls to follow him.
This definition of God's power reverses human ideas of what constitutes poverty, weakness, persecution, self-sacrifice.

IMPLICATIONS

Jesus' trip to Jerusalem is itself an embodiment of God's power.
God's power can be known firsthand only by those willing to give up their own power.
God's power is a function of God's mercy, not the reverse (Mark 10:17, 27).
The dialogue offers an understanding of the kinds of miracles that are greatest.

REACTIONS

Judged by this definition of God's power, most current Christian ideas of power are at best sub-Christian.
The story should suggest that we ask in all seriousness what would happen if we accepted this view of God's power as reliable.

A MEDITATION

Blaise Pascal, *Pensées*, trans. A.J. Krailsheimer (New York: Penguin Books, 1968), thought 555.

38 Help Wanted!

TEXT Jesus: The harvest is abundant but the workers are scarce; so pray the Master of the harvest to send workers into his harvest. (Matt. 9:37–38)

SITUATION Matthew 9:35–38; Luke 10:1–2
A chief shepherd sends disciples as shepherds to the lost sheep of Israel.

CONVICTIONS God is master of the harvest; it belongs to him.
God needs human harvesters to reap the harvest.
Jesus is such a messenger/shepherd/harvester.
This is a call, not for volunteers, but for prayers to God.

ASSUMPTIONS The text visualizes a chain of generations of harvesters: Jesus, disciples, future
answers to prayer.
Harvesting embraces many activities: proclaiming, teaching, exorcising, healing.
Prayers recognize that God is the beginning and the end of the task of
harvesting/shepherding.

IMPLICATIONS God can become known through the action of the harvesters.
Harvesting includes the gift of God's peace and the anticipation of God's
judgment.
The image of final judgment is here fused with the image of gathering God's
harvest.
The disciples' compassion is traced back to Jesus' compassion and thence to
God's compassion.

QUESTIONS How can a story so time-bound as this be correlated to the occupational
structures of twentieth-century society?
Are the ancient metaphors of shepherding and harvesting still viable?

FOOD FOR THOUGHT Kroner, *How Do We Know God?* pp. 61-70.

39 Peace Work

TEXT

Jesus: Blessed are the peacemakers, for they shall be called sons of God.

(Matt. 5:9)

SITUATION

Matthew 5:1–12; 10:13; John 14:27; Hebrews 12:14
The basic mandate that disciples should relay to followers
Preparation for persecution (Matt. 5:10–12)

CONVICTIONS

The text focuses on God's relation to disciples; it indicates an action that
simultaneously creates sonship and fatherhood. As the God of peace, he
makes peace through the obedience of peacemakers.

The text also focuses on God's relationship to persecutors of the disciples,
their enemies and his. Disciples become sons by sharing with these
enemies God's offer of reconciliation.

ASSUMPTIONS

The disclosure of God as a peace-seeker is conveyed through a chain of
human revealers: Jesus, disciples, crowds, persecutors.
To belong to this chain is considered a highest good—sonship.
To accept suffering for others is considered a major form of peacemaking.
Jesus fills a multiple role as Son, mediator of sonship, example of
peacemaking, source of blessedness.

IMPLICATIONS

The beatitude is a hidden warning against disciples who because of
persecution shun their duty of mediating God's peace to the persecutors.
Peacemaking makes disciples the successors of the prophets (Matt. 5:12).
The bond between the Father and peacemaking is fully actual; the bond
between human beings and peacemaking is only potential, but it is no
less decisive.

A MYSTERY

What is there about God's relationship to human beings that creates a
situation in which only peacemakers can become his sons and only they
can learn to know him as their Father? Where does this begetting take
place? How is this bond forged?

PURITY AND SUFFERING

Miguel de Unamuno, *The Tragic Sense of Life*, trans. J.E. Crawford Flitch
(1921; reprint, New York: Dover Publications, 1954), ch. 9 (last 10 pp., on
the scandal of the cross and the suffering of God).

40   Who Scatters This Flock?

TEXT   Jesus: You will all fall away; for it is written, "I [God] will strike the shepherd [me], and the sheep [you] will be scattered." But after I am raised up, I will go before you to Galilee. (Mark:14:27–28)

SITUATION   Mark 14:26–28; Matthew 26:30–32
On the Mount of Olives, just before Jesus' arrest

CONVICTIONS   In the citation from Zechariah, God is speaking as the one who strikes the shepherd; this makes God responsible for Jesus' death.
God is therefore also responsible for scattering the sheep, i.e., for the disciples' fear-driven flight from the cross.
As yet, the disciples do not believe in this God because all of them have promised not to fall away (Mark 14:31).
Yet, God's statement is verified: all do fall away (vs. 50).

ASSUMPTIONS   God knows the disciples better than they know themselves.
God's act of scattering them does not diminish their culpability for gross self-deception.
God's act of scattering them is in line with the intention to gather them later.
God's act of striking the shepherd is also necessary for a later raising up that will lead to the disciples' mission.

IMPLICATIONS   Jesus' knowledge of God and the disciples' ignorance of God are by implication a part of Mark's interpretation of the Last Supper (14:22–25).
Peter's blindness now and his vision later underscore the contrast between discipular self-confidence and repentance.
God's plan in such events as crucifixion are of a sort that only Jesus can recognize and only he can reveal.

REACTIONS   Who can really believe in a god who kills the shepherd and scatters the sheep in his own flock? Who can really follow a shepherd who teaches that God acts in such a way? God could have treated the shepherds and the sheep better than that (Mark 14:36; Matt. 26:53).

BACKGROUND   Zechariah 13—14

41   The Disciples' New Clothes

TEXT

Jesus: Listen! I am sending the promise of my Father to you; but stay in the city until you are clothed with power from on high. (Luke 24:49)

SITUATION

Luke 24:44–49
The Risen Lord speaking to his disciples in Jerusalem.
This vision becomes the basis for their commission and for their power to announce repentance and forgiveness to all nations.

CONVICTIONS

God promised the gift of the Spirit, which would convey authority to offer forgiveness of sins to all nations (Acts 1:8; 2:16–21).
As Jesus' Father, God now gives Jesus the authority to mediate this gift.
The text traces the gift of this new power: from God to Jesus to the Apostles to all nations. God may be found either by tracing this power to its source or by observing it at work.

ASSUMPTIONS

This gift is the conclusion of all that had happened before the cross: the Scriptures, the story of Israel, the birth stories in Luke, the earlier training of the Apostles.
The gift is also a concentration of all that happened before Luke's account: visions and auditions of the living Master, the commission from him, the response of Jews and Gentiles to the message.
The text views the Apostles' work as a point at which God's blessing of their work intersects with their blessing of God through that work.
The text focuses attention upon all that happens when God's enemies repent for having crucified Jesus and when God forgives them.

IMPLICATIONS

"My Father" indicates the unique role of Jesus as God's Son and the unique revelation, through Jesus, of God as Jesus' Father.
The task of theology is to make intelligible the inner linkages between the leading actors: God, Spirit, Son, Apostles.
In this task, the experience of repentance and forgiveness supplies important hermeneutical clues.
All this is implicit in faith in Jesus as the one through whom God offers repentance and forgiveness.

QUESTION

How can a modern person hold all this in mind while pondering the question whether or not to believe in God?

AN ANSWER

Wilhelm Stählin, *The Mystery of God* (London: SCM Press, 1937), pp. 15–23.

42   God Transfers His Authority

TEXT

Jesus: All authority in heaven and on earth has been given to me. Go therefore and make disciples of all nations, baptizing them in the name of the Father and of the Son and of the Holy Spirit, teaching them to observe all that I have commanded you. See, I am with you always, to the close of the age.

(Matt. 28:18–20)

SITUATION

Matthew 28:16–20
In Matthew, the only words spoken by the Risen Lord to the disciples, in which he gives them their instructions.

CONVICTIONS

God wields all authority in heaven and on earth.
God has shared this authority with Jesus.
This authority is now conferred on the eleven disciples; it covers their mission to all nations until the close of the age.
Through being baptized and obeying Jesus' commands, others will be brought under this rule of authority.

ASSUMPTIONS

The gift of authority presupposes Jesus' death and resurrection and describes what happened in those events.
The assumed distance between heaven and earth is permanently bridged by this transfer of authority.
Jesus sets a triple condition for the transfer: going, baptizing, teaching.
This commission, with the continuing presence of the Risen Lord, makes the exercise of his authority dependent on obedience to his commands.

IMPLICATIONS

The reaction of doubt is always possible (vs. 17).
The worship of Jesus provides a native habitat for recognizing this revelation.
This mountain is connected symbolically to many other mountains in Scripture.
The exercise of authority is bound up with "the Name."

REACTIONS

How can such a momentary act as baptism become the channel for such great authority?
Does Matthew mean that this presence of Jesus in the future (vs. 20) is a fulfillment of the angel's word in the beginning (1:23)?

THOUGHTS ON RESURRECTION-LANGUAGE

Caird, *Language and Imagery of the Bible*, pp. 211–18.

A Collage of Images

Having examined some forty episodes in Jesus' training of his intern-prophets, you should be in a position to scan the panorama of images in the Gospels to observe patterns of thinking that recur frequently enough to demand attention. In noting these patterns, I do not wish to prejudice your reactions or to recommend my own theological stance. I simply wish to urge you to pause in your analysis of separate items to ponder the cumulative impact.

One recurrent feature, for example, is the way in which the Gospels stress the degree to which Jesus' disciples failed to understand or to share Jesus' basic convictions about God. In this respect the narratives reflect an inherent realism. The theological distance between Jesus and his first followers gives silent but impressive witness to the uniqueness of his thinking about God and to the difficulties implicit in that thinking. In view of this distance it should not surprise us that modern readers find many of the same convictions incomprehensible, if not reprehensible. We gain nothing by ignoring or minimizing the distance between our own conceptions of the Deity and those embodied in the Gospels. A recognition of that distance is a necessity for achieving clarity and honesty.

Another recurrent feature of these texts is the tendency to speak of God by the use of verbs instead of nouns, not in terms of who God is but of what he does. Of such verbs there is an almost unlimited profusion and diversity. God is one who

speaks and listens	sees and is seen
gets and gives	blesses and curses
promises and threatens	rewards and punishes
gathers and scatters	reveals and hides
brings in and casts out	forgives and condemns
builds and destroys	plants and harvests
calls and sends	seeks and finds
rules and judges	sends peace and a sword
attacks and defends	hastens and delays
heals and harms	gives life and kills

Why this reliance on verbs of action? All of them imply that God is to be known through what he does. All imply that not only is God's activity comparable to human activity but also that it is somehow coordinated with the daily behavior of quite ordinary individuals. What should we infer from these linguistic features? Do they indicate where we should look for evidences of God's presence and power? Should they reverse our tendency to think of God in terms of God's governance of nations and planets, rather than governance of minds and hearts? Should the frequent reference to God's threats and curses correct current language habits that speak and think only in terms of blessing and loving? At the very least, the array of verbs suggests new ranges of meaning in the traditional attributes of deity: *omniscience, omnipresence, omnipotence*. The God of the Gospels is much more human than those *omni*-words imply.

In addition to the verbs, one notes, of course, the use of many nouns in reference to the Deity: *farmer, builder, owner, creator, shepherd, commander-in-chief, judge, scourge of demons, dispatcher of angels*. Among these images, three seem most frequent and typical: God is thought of as one who sends, as one who rules, and as one who is Father. Study of each of these metaphors should be productive.

God is often spoken of as the one who has sent Jesus, a messenger who, in turn, sends disciples in a chain that reaches the current audience. God's call evokes a coming; God's sending evokes a going. God's invisible action becomes visible through the coming and going of the messengers. Accordingly, we encounter a twin image: the metaphor of the Sender and the sent. The bond between the Divine Sender and the person sent is assumed to be so intimate that any response to either constitutes a response to the other. To speak of God as the Sender is to speak in the language of metaphor; yet to the one who is sent, nothing could be more real. The messenger has an overwhelming sense of being addressed by an Other. The invisibility of the Other is such that the response can emerge only from within the deepest recesses of the self. Thus the reality of the Sender becomes inseparable from each messenger's awareness of vocation. The call and the commission define the beginning and the end of that messenger's existence. Initial resistance to the call only deepens its certainty when that resistance has been overcome. Yet the messenger can present no external credentials of the commission. It is not surprising, then, that the messenger's audience should experience the same resistance and, once that resistance is overcome, should experience the same inner compulsions. At each step in the process, the response to the messenger conceals or discloses a response to the One who has sent the representative. Knowledge of God as sender is thus conveyed through the self-knowledge of the audiences. So from the chain's first link to its current messenger, the cogency of the twin image Sender/sent stems from the heart's response to the voice of messengers who claim to have been sent from this particular but invisible Sender. Such observations as these seem to be required by the texts that have been examined. Theologians who do not recognize the role of God as sender may well be dealing with quite another deity and with another symbolic universe.

A second twin metaphor that recurs frequently is that of King/kingdom. God is recognized as king by those who, in response to his invitation, enter his kingdom. There is, of course, a close correlation between this and the former image. The one who sends is King; the one whom he sends announces the approach of his kingdom. Acceptance of that messenger is tantamount to entering the kingdom. The basic message that binds the Sender first to the messengers and then to their audiences is this: the realm where God is king has come near to you (Luke 10:9). In the former image we observed the chain of knowledge reaching back from the audience through the messengers to the Sender. Now we notice a similar chain that links the power and authority and glory of the King to those messengers, who through obedience become heirs and citizens of the kingdom. One cannot accept such a messenger without welcoming the kingdom that the messenger announces. The announcement of the dawning of the kingdom is as uncertain/certain as the claim that a particular messenger has been sent from this Sender. In both cases, the response involves a leap of faith within the hearts of those addressed.

Now we must notice a similar correlation between these two images—Sender/sent and King/kingdom—and a third—that of Father/family. The Sender is the King is the Father; those who are sent inherit his kingdom as children of this parent. In Jesus' training of his disciples, this master image of the family is undoubtedly the most frequent and the most central. The texts indicate that the image becomes operative in many different ways. This deity becomes the Father, these children become his children, in human actions that respond to, rely upon, and reflect divine activity:

> where God's command elicits obedience
> where his love of enemies engenders prayers for persecutors
> where being forgiven prompts forgiveness
> where his peace empowers peacemaking
> where a call to repent elicits repentance
> where his creation of a pure heart induces honesty
> where his faithfulness produces faithfulness under stress.

The two metaphors, father and family, are interactive and interdependent; they come into operation simultaneously. Where God's Word is heard and obeyed, there it becomes necessary, logically as well as linguistically, to describe the invisible linkage in terms of filial and familial relationships.

In none of the texts do Evangelists use this twin image to refer to God and all humanity. Nor do the metaphors indicate a permanently secure status for all members of the family, as if those born by obedience as God's children retain that status whatever they may do later. A present tense governs this relationship; the Father's family is composed of those, and only those, who now both hear and obey his command.

The twinning of the metaphors shows how closely theology and ethics are bound in such a pattern of thinking. The usual practice is to separate thinking about God (theology) from thinking about human behavior (ethics). But in the Gospels these two can be separated no more easily than denying the bond between parent and children. The father cannot exist apart from his family, nor the family apart from the father. Whenever the father acts, the children act; their visible obedience is their testimony to the invisible parentage. Theology and ethics are as inseparable in reality as in the grammar of the metaphors.

This correlation may be detected, for example, when we analyze the experience of forgiving and being forgiven. To forgive an enemy is to act as a child of God; that action is linked directly to God's action in being a father (i.e., in forgiving). Contrariwise, for a child of God to refuse to forgive an enemy is to guarantee the wrath of the Father (i.e., he ceases to be a father). So in acting mercifully, God's children activate the twin metaphor that describes the reciprocal relationship. The beatitude comes into effect: "Blessed are the merciful, for their Father will be merciful to them" (Matt. 5:7). That beatitude is neither an example of wishful thinking nor a vague postponement of reward into the future; it is a declaration of the truth about the Father/family relationship. It is a revelation of the double authorship of the same action.

This metaphorical language helps to explain another feature of the texts: they assert the authority of the Father in an absolute, uncompromising way and the obligation of the children with equal rigor and finality. "Unless you deny yourselves, take up the cross and follow me, you cannot be my disciples." The intrinsic definition of Fatherhood/family fuses the unlimited authority of the one and the unqualified obedience of the other. Each attribute assigned to the Parent (e.g., love of enemies) assigns to the family a corresponding duty. The truth of the metaphors is sealed in the hidden recesses of the heart from which that double assignment springs. The true test of all sonship is indicated by the Gethsemane prayer, "Not my will but yours be done." Here there can be no shading of grays, only black and white. Here thought does not dare to take refuge in the shaded areas of pragmatic compromise. The sharp lines in this etching of the human situation, its apparent arbitrariness and absoluteness, are dictated by logic and grammar, both of which would be destroyed by any suggestion of partial obedience to a partial authority. The relations of Father and family become the true magnetic poles of a universe that make dependable compass readings possible.

In recent years the Father/sons metaphor has become offensive to many readers as evidence of male chauvinism in the Bible. This perception has led to extensive efforts to eliminate both terms from translations and lectionary readings. How do the texts that have been examined bear on this issue? It may be noted that none of the texts explicitly refers to sex. That is to say, the masculine sex is not essential to the meaning, no more than the figure of a king is essential to a monarchical form of earthly government. God's Word, obedience to which marks one's birth as God's child, can be described in maternal as well as paternal language (cf. text 7). The Divine Parent becomes parent only when a command is obeyed, as when an act of mercy prompts a responding mercy. In the Gospels, as in the Epistles (e.g., Gal. 3:28), thought transcends differences in sex among members of this embassy, kingdom, or family. The conversation between God and the heart of each disciple proceeds at a level deeper than the level of awareness of sex, whether the sex of God, of Christ, or of a disciple. Whoever is not aware of that deeper level at which the terms *male* and *female* become irrelevant has not been emancipated from sex discrimination. To avoid the Gospel terms *Father* and *Son* because of masculinity would be to misunderstand the structures of biblical language, logic, and thought.

It is characteristic of the Gospels that thought shifts very easily from one image to another. An example is the shift from flock to family to kingdom in the assurance "Fear not, little flock, for it is your Father's good pleasure to give you the kingdom" (Luke 13:32). Thus it is possible to correct false inferences from one image by thinking of the others. If one infers from the Sender/sent image that the focus falls on the response of individuals only, such a false inference is corrected by the communal character of the kingdom and family. Or one might infer from the use of the King/kingdom image that a primary connotation is that of space and time (e.g., the kingdom is either here or there, either now or then). Yet the conjunction with the embassy and family images corrects this impression. The kingdom is no more space-specific or time-specific than are the embassy or family metaphors; all are strongly vocation-specific, a vocation that applies to the entire community and to each of its members. By the same logic, the image of Father/family is no more sex-specific than are the parallel images.

In this workbook you have already seen that the reliance on metaphors such as these results in basic changes in the entire language. Ordinary words are used to point to quite extraordinary relationships.

> Jesus: None of you has left house or brothers or sisters or mother or father or children or lands for my sake and for the gospel who will not receive a hundredfold now in this time—houses and brothers and sisters and mothers and children and lands—with persecutions—and in the age to come, eternal life. But many that are first will be last, and the last first. (Mark 10:29–31)

House, mother, sister, land, first, last: none of these words is new or technical. All are simple words, the common coin of illiterate people in every culture. Yet they now bear new meanings, accessible only to the newly literate. When the *last* has come to mean the *first*, those two words can never again be the same. What does the term *home* mean after one home has been left and a hundred homes have been made accessible? As the family of a hundred sisters is different from a family with three, so the very term *sister* loses some connotations and gains others. In this text the reference to persecution purges the new language of sentimentality and preciosity.

This change in vocabulary is by no means limited to a few words. The texts involve radical changes in the meanings of more than fifty words:

rich and poor	strong and weak
shame and glory	lowliness and exaltation
sorrow and joy	lost and found
old and new	slave and lord
day and night	watching and sleeping
evil and good	small and great
near and far	blessing and curse
innocent and guilty	sinner and righteous
peace and war	captive and free
God and Satan	death and life

When so many key words receive such new cargoes, the very structure of language is affected; behind those changes in linguistic structure one can sense changes in perceptions of what is real and what is illusory, along with changes in the resulting patterns of thought. Those changes lie behind the Gospel distinctions between the *wise* and the *babes* (Matt. 11:25); that is, the wise are those who, hearing the proclamation of God's kingdom, are unable to free themselves from their habits of thought and language. The babes are those who prove to have the requisite flexibility.

However that may be, the texts impel us to ask why God should have revealed himself to babes, not to the wise. Was it because the wise had learned to think of God's presence as somehow separated from the contrite individual by the archetypal saga of creation, by the ancient election of Israel, by the tumultuous history of the nation since the Exodus and the Exile, by the extensiveness of the Torah and its multiple demands, by the automatic procession of temple festivals and sacrifices, by the professional roles of priests and scribes, by the unbroken routines of public prayers and fasting? Was it because the babes were predisposed to think of God as speaking directly to the humbled heart that had despaired of direct access to forgiveness and healing? Did this prepare babes to respond immediately to the unexpected announcement of good news, with its trenchant warning but miraculous promise, as uttered by messengers who claimed to speak with the authority of the God of Abraham, Isaac, and Jacob? Did the new awareness of God's invasion of the heart and the gracious gift of the kingdom enable them to grasp the patterns of thought and speech that were indigenous to the new realm? However we may answer such questions, the texts provide evidence that members of this new flock/family/kingdom/embassy began to adapt their language to the God-logic that was native to that realm.

An example of the change in linguistic habits is provided by the image of the kingdom of God. A study of this image has been central to the twentieth-century study of the New Testament, a study on which scholars are far from consensus. This study, however, has unearthed three new clues to an understanding of this phrase. The first clue stresses priority. Before asking about the kingdom, we should ask about the God to whom it belongs and who brings it near to those addressed by God's spokespersons. The term *kingdom* is a metaphor whose basic coordinates are the presence, the authority, the power, the glory, the invasive will, of a quite specific deity. Changes in thinking about those coordinates inevitably produce changes in the term *kingdom*. A second clue has to do with the language. *Kingdom* is only half of a twin metaphor; it can be understood only in connection with its twin, that is, its heirs. This metaphor fulfills functions similar to those of the other compound metaphors, e.g., father/family, healer/healed, master/slaves. A third clue has to do with the point at which the interpreter of the kingdom is standing. Is this the point at which God reveals himself to babes, not to the wise, the point at which repentance helps the helpless to welcome the good news, the point at which the hundredth sheep rejoices with the shepherd? The Gospel references to the kingdom are indigenous to the language of this family and no other.

Among many changes in vocabulary none were more decisive than the terms referring to God, illustrating the truth that for those who live in a world where the love of God is in fact the first commandment, every change in God-logic affects everything else. This may be illustrated by text 31, the parable of the Pharisee and the tax collector. Of course that parable does not describe the homecoming of the tax collector, but his joy on returning from the temple should not be minimized. He is a person who has viewed God and God's judgment with absolute respect; otherwise he would not have gone to the temple in the first place. He is also one for whom his status as a sinner has become a source of despair, barring him not only from God's presence but from good standing in Israel. He seems to have agreed with the Pharisee's judgment on that matter; otherwise his prayer would not have been such a staccato cry wrenched from the heart. To him, God's answer to that prayer must have seemed miraculous. When he went home, taking God's justification with him, God must have seemed different and he himself also different because God had altered his status. He could then understand the stories of the healing of the blind and the cleansing of the lepers. In the same way the joy of the shepherd over finding the lost sheep was a source of joy for the hundredth sheep that was found. The new language about God released volcanic enthusiasms among those whose self-image had been transformed by God's actions. Jesus had healed their blindness and deafness. Such enthusiasm was itself an index of the new God-logic.

A similar index appeared in the depth of hostility aroused by the same logic. From Jesus' first appearance in the hometown synagogue to his execution on a hill outside Jerusalem's walls, he aroused deep hostility among the leaders of synagogue and temple. I am convinced that the root of this intense conflict must have been centered in his convictions about God. After all, these adversaries were the exponents and defenders of Israel's knowledge of God. It was their own appointment to teach and to defend such knowledge that prompted them to reject the theological position of Jesus. We cannot comprehend either side of this conflict unless we comprehend the other.

The next section contains the texts in which Jesus addressed his adversaries. That conflict is treated further after an examination of the texts.

JESUS
AND
HIS ADVERSARIES

JESUS
AND
HIS ADVERSARIES

A simple but sure test of obedience to the first commandment is this: does a change in the picture of God change everything else . . . or nothing else?

The Gospels are agreed on one important point: it was to the lost sheep of the house of Israel that God sent Jesus as shepherd. His assignment was to invite fellow Jews into the kingdom of God, long promised to the heirs of Abraham. So fully did Jesus accept this assignment that later Gentile Christians have often been troubled by so narrow a definition of God's plan. But the Gospels leave no doubt that this was, in fact, Jesus' target. To be sure, one may find in the records significant exceptions, as when Jesus answered the desperate cry of a woman from Syria. But these exceptions are rare, and many of them are designed as object lessons to Jesus' primary audience, Israel. In basic thrust, then, the Gospel writers were radically pro-Semitic. Thus we must draw within the range of our vision some twenty episodes in which Jesus spoke of God in connection with his encounters with adversaries within Israel.

Jesus himself, of course, was a Jew, not a Christian. It was from Israel that he called his first disciples. He and they became, in biblical idiom, a sword of division. In a more recent idiom the audience was polarized whenever he or they were present in synagogue or temple. Luke stressed such polarization in his account of the first keynote address in the Nazareth synagogue: "all were filled with wrath" (4:28). In this section the texts are in complete agreement in identifying Jesus' adversaries. They were the recognized spokespersons of God in Israel, the leaders in synagogue and temple, variously described as scribes, lawyers, Pharisees, Sadducees, priests, the high priest. Their typical reaction was to reject Jesus' claim to be a successor to Moses, Elijah, or Elisha. Jesus, in turn, accepted that rejection as an expression of God's will, intrinsic to his mission. Hostility emerged at the beginning of his work and developed in steady crescendo until the crucifixion. One can find very little evidence that any other group was moved to such deadly hostility. At the end, to be sure, the Roman governor and soldiers were implicated, but only after the Son of man had been betrayed by his own people into the hands of the Gentiles.

In our own time this history has been subject to drastic revision in order to eliminate evidence that various groups considered obnoxious. As always, such censorship tells more about the censors than about the original events. Some interpreters, moved by animosity toward modern Jews, are eager to identify them with the "Christ-killers" and to use the Gospels as support for their vendettas, oblivious to the character of Jesus' mission as it embodied the will of Jesus' Father. Others seek to destroy the biblical basis for such anti-Semitism by minimizing the scriptural evidence of antagonism between this Jewish Messiah and his Jewish foes. One familiar move is to attribute this antagonism to the Evangelists, relieving Jesus himself of any responsibility for it. The Gospels were written, so the argument goes, during a period of acute persecution of the church by the Roman authorities. To reduce the risk of martyrdom, the Gospel writers shifted the basic guilt for Jesus' death from the Romans to the Jews. The result has been centuries of Christian retribution against Jews. Often the efforts of censors are less sweeping, as, for example, a 1986 news report of a church in New York City. The pastor revised the liturgy for Good Friday to avoid anti-Semitic references. John 19:15 no longer reads "The Jews cried out, 'Away with him, away with him,'" but instead it reads "The crowd took up the chant, 'crucify him, crucify him.'" Censors are seldom aware that they are the ones who suffer most from such innocent-sounding revisions of history. The conflicts between Jesus and his opponents cannot so easily be erased from the records.

Before examining those records, however, I think that several comments may be relevant to this issue. First of all, we must question the assumption that today's churches and synagogues, as religious communities, are lineal descendants of Jesus and his disciples on the one hand and of the ancient Pharisees on the other. This assumption is based on extreme literalism, as in the aphorism "Once a Christian, always a Christian; once a Jew, always a Jew." It was reliance on this assumption that caused much of the original turmoil described in the Gospels. Both John the Baptist and Jesus believed that God is able to raise up sons of Abraham out of stones. Both challenged the tendency to define Israel by racial or religious inheritance. The Gospels relay the good news of an emancipation from all rigid boundaries that separate one religious community from all others.

Many revisionists ignore another fact—the clear evidence that it was God's will that Jesus and his first disciples should carry on their work within Israel, within synagogues where they gathered for worship with their neighbors, and within the temple where they celebrated the annual festivals. To be sure, the Gospels describe their debates as a way by which Jesus cast fire on the earth (Luke 12:49). But these debates took place within the same household; they appealed to the same Scriptures and recognized loyalty to the same first commandment. Jesus' controversy with his people was no more sharp than that of earlier prophets such as Jeremiah; but as in Jeremiah's day, the debate proceeded between one group of Jews and the others. Had this debate not led to the competition between two separate religions, Jesus would never have been regarded as more anti-Semitic than Jeremiah.

Why should these messengers have been sent to this people? The Gospels indicate an answer: to express God's love for them, a love that Jesus shared. The acceptance of persecution was an index of the strength of the love. Apart from persecution, God's love for persecutors could not be demonstrated. For example, it was as an enemy of God that Paul discovered the power of God's love for such enemies as himself (Rom. 5:1–5). It was in the line of duty, in the line of his mission to his opponents, that Jesus was killed by them. This is why the Gospels developed a unique language for describing God's relation to Israel, a mission that turned all people into adversaries so that the call to repentance might become relevant to all (cf. Rom. 11:32). By his love for the messianic people, the Messiah called them to repent and to take the narrow road into God's kingdom (Luke 19:41–44). Few revisionists have learned to speak the language of the Gospels. They do not recognize the reasons why, if the Gospels find the Jewish adversaries more culpable than the Romans, the Gospels also hold Jesus' disciples still more culpable than his adversaries, more culpable for their ignorance and obtuseness, their fears and ambitions, their denials and betrayals. I make such comments here to urge you to separate the historical problem from the contemporary one. It is not by censoring the ancient story that we best come to terms with the modern issue.

In the material that follows, my intention is to bring to the surface the multiple encounters between Jesus and the leaders of his people and to analyze the degree to which different perceptions of God were involved in those collisions. In meeting this objective I have found it desirable to change the format in two places. First, we can dispense with the category *assumptions* because those features in the thought-structures have been adequately covered in Section 1. Thus we can move directly from the *convictions* about God to the *implications* stemming from those convictions. Second, instead of *reactions*, the study will focus upon *issues*. In the earlier pages the goal has been to prompt you to voice your own problems or objections to the outlook of the Gospels. In the following pages, under the heading of issues, the goal is to formulate as precisely as possible what it was in the ancient situation that induced Jesus' opponents to decide to destroy him. Recalling these issues, you may well find yourselves agreeing not with Jesus but with his adversaries. Whether or not that is so, it should be a test of your wits to ponder why both sides held so tenaciously to their opposing positions. Sooner or later these following questions must be answered: Was the tragic outcome of the struggle traceable to two opposing conceptions of the same God? Were the two ways of thinking about God so exclusive of each other as to make that outcome inevitable? Was the cross the inevitable result of loyalties to two competing gods? To what extent did the conflict reflect the use of two radically different language structures, two vocabularies that gave contrary meanings to the same words? Did the two groups reside in two metaphorical worlds in which life in one would mean death in the other? Perhaps a study of the situation will enable us to recover those two contradictory God-logics.

TEXTS

43   God Heals a Syrian General

TEXT

Jesus went to the synagogue. . . . The book of the prophet Isaiah was given to him. . . . "The spirit of the Lord is upon me, because he has anointed me." . . . All in the synagogue were filled with wrath. (Luke 4:16–18, 28)

SITUATION

Luke 4:16–30
Jesus' keynote address in Nazareth's synagogue where he announces the fulfillment of Isaiah's prophecy

CONVICTIONS
Can you subtract from or add to these?

God has sent Jesus, anointing him Messiah to set his people free.
This fulfillment matches God's earlier promises to Israel.
God's gift of the Spirit enables Jesus to speak with authority and to act with God's power.
God's healing continues the works of Elijah, Elisha, and their successors.
Those healings show God's preference for a helpless alien woman and a powerful Gentile general.
The worshipers are enraged by this attitude toward Israel's enemies.

IMPLICATIONS
Subtract from or add others to these four.

The fact that Jesus stood in the synagogue implies that his references to Israel's enemies were designed for the sake of Israel.
His adversaries heard a message quite different from Isaiah's. They detected nothing in the prophet to show that God's acceptable year had dawned.
Through Jesus' activity, God was defining the true purpose of the sabbath, Scripture, synagogue, Israel, worship.
Luke saw this scene as predictive of the final clash on Golgotha. Jesus was governed by the Spirit; his adversaries were governed by denial that their God would heal an enemy general and that the synagogue was the place for such a message.

ISSUES
If you had been a Pharisee, are those the questions you would have raised? What other questions would you have raised?

Who was best qualified to interpret Isaiah and to interpret current events in the light of Isaiah—trained scholars or this unknown prophet?
Did God no longer give Israel any priority over Sidonian widows and enemy generals?
Was God in fact so partial to the groups mentioned by Jesus?
Where could one find any convincing evidence that this was God's acceptable year?

BACKGROUND

Isaiah 1

44 Only God Is Good

TEXT

A man, running up and kneeling before Jesus: Good teacher, what must I do to inherit eternal life?

Jesus: Why do you call me good? No one is good but God alone.

(Mark 10:17–18)

SITUATION

Mark 10:17–22; Matthew 19:16–22; Luke 18:18–30; Romans 3:9–20

Dialogue between Jesus and a potential disciple—a rich man (Matt., "young man"; Luke, "a ruler"). En route to Jerusalem and the cross, Jesus uses the episode as a lesson for disciples.

CONVICTIONS

At what points do those views differ from the questioner's?

God is good.

Only God is good.

God's goodness excludes all human pretensions and claims to goodness.

God's goodness is expressed in commands on how to inherit life.

Obedience to these commands requires poverty and excludes wealth.

IMPLICATIONS

Which of those implications was most controversial?

It is wrong to let estimates of human goodness displace the recognition of God's goodness.

Being a teacher or inheriting life is not the same as becoming good.

God rejects the law when it is used as a means of achieving superior goodness.

To become Jesus' disciple does not convey goodness. Discipleship equals the willingness to join Jesus in moving in the opposite direction—downward, not upward (See Phil. 2:6–11).

ISSUES

Are the major issues doctrinal or ethical? Are they motivational or emotional or vocational?

How could teachers in Israel shift their goal from becoming good (and therefore better than others) to becoming poor (and therefore rich in heaven)?

Does limiting goodness to God undercut the reasons why synagogue teachers became teachers?

Can a god who commands such sacrifice be considered good?

In what ways did this teacher and Jesus teach different views of God, of goodness, of eternal life and how to obtain it?

ON PERSPECTIVES

Karl Barth, *The Epistle to the Romans*, 6th ed., trans. Edwin C. Hoskyns (London: Oxford University Press, 1968), ch. 11, comment on Romans 11:1–6.

45   The God-Neighbor Syndrome

TEXT

A scribe: Which commandment is first of all?
Jesus: Hear, O Israel, the Lord our God, the Lord is one.
      You shall love the Lord your God with all your heart. . . .
      You shall love your neighbor as yourself. (Mark 12:28–31)

SITUATION

Mark 12:28–34; Matthew 22:34–40; Luke 10:25–28; Deuteronomy 6:4,5;
    Leviticus 19:18
A debate in the temple near the close of Jesus' ministry

CONVICTIONS

The Lord is one.
The one Lord is the God of Israel, to whom Israel belongs.
Oneness requires total obedience, "all your heart."
Oneness of God, of Israel, of heart, includes love of neighbor.
Jesus identifies himself with this command concerning "*our* God."

IMPLICATIONS

Agreement on this command brings Jesus and the scribes close together
    (Mark 12:32–34).
Mark's readers would have found clear evidence here of Jesus' loyalty to
    God and to Israel.
They would have seen the possibility of support from the scribes.
Luke's readers would have seen failure of Israel's leaders to link the love of
    God to love of neighbor.
The text focuses attention on the oneness of Israel's heart more than on the
    oneness of the Lord.

ISSUES

Given this agreement on central issues (God, Israel, Scripture), the text
    suggests potential points of conflict (identity of neighbor, understanding
    of love, the linkage between God/Israel/neighbor, the role of offerings
    and sacrifices, the bearing that the commandment has on scribal practice)
    (Mark 12:38–40).
How is formal orthodoxy of belief related to daily conduct vis-à-vis others?
How is the agreement on the greatest commandment related to scribal
    participation in Jesus' crucifixion?
How does Israel move toward loving the one Lord with one heart?

ON THE MEANING OF ONENESS

Martin Buber, *I and Thou*, trans. and ed. Walter Kaufman (New York:
Charles Scribner's Sons, 1970), part 1 (pp. 53–87), part 3 (pp. 123–33).

46   A Den of Robbers

TEXT   They came to Jerusalem. . . . [Jesus] entered the temple. . . . "Is it not written, 'My [God's] house shall be called a house of prayer for all the nations [Gentiles]'? But you [priests and scribes] have made it a den of robbers." And the chief priests and the scribes . . . sought a way to destroy him.

(Mark 11:15, 17–18)

SITUATION   Mark 11:15–19; Matthew 21:12–13; Luke 19:45–48; John 2:13–17; Isaiah 56:7; Jeremiah 7:11

Jesus' final visit to Jerusalem and his final break with temple authorities

CONVICTIONS   God speaks to Israel through the Scriptures but also through Jesus' words and deeds as interpretations of Scripture.

God claims the temple as his house and therefore as a place of prayer for Gentiles as well as for Israel.

God's appointed stewards have stolen this house from God and from the Gentiles.

Their action places them in opposition to God, the Scriptures, the people of God, the Gentiles, and the true temple.

These robbers fear the people more than they fear God (Mark 11:18).

IMPLICATIONS   Jesus takes the initiative in defense of God's house in his attack on the robbers.

Jesus claims that God prefers Gentile prayers to Jewish sacrifices, for which these sales were necessary.

God's temple is not to be found within this den of robbers. Thus Jesus' deeds as well as his words meant the destruction of the temple of these robbers.

The story of the fig tree symbolizes God's destruction of their "temple."

ISSUES   This episode forces participants and readers to make a final choice between Jesus and his adversaries.

To accept Jesus as God's agent requires radical changes in temple sacrifices, income, organization, objectives, the priesthood.

Jesus' following is large enough to make this choice necessary in political terms. (Mark 11:18).

By quoting Scripture, Jesus makes the decision a decision between his Bible and theirs, his God and theirs.

BACKGROUND   Jeremiah 7

47 God or Beelzebul?

TEXT

A blind and dumb demoniac was brought to Jesus and he healed him.
The Pharisees: It is only by Beelzebul, the prince of demons, that this man casts out demons.
Jesus: If it is by the Spirit of God that I cast out demons, then the kingdom of God has come upon you. (Matt. 12:22, 24, 28)

SITUATION

Matthew 12:22–28; Luke 11:14–23; Mark 3:22–27
A debate over how Jesus' exorcisms should be explained

CONVICTIONS

The ultimate enemies are Satan and God and their two kingdoms.
The power that enabled Jesus to exorcise demons came from God.
This power is a sign of the intrusion of God's authority into the situation.
The alternate explanation, Satan's power, is impossible, because that would pit Satan against Satan and would signal a fall of Satan's kingdom.
In choosing to oppose Jesus, the scribes and the Pharisees have chosen to be against God and for Satan.

IMPLICATIONS

Jesus' opponents have been guilty of blasphemy aganst the Holy Spirit and must face God's judgment as progeny of snakes, i.e., Satan (cf. Matt. 12:31–37).
As Jesus' words are a channel of God's power, so the Pharisees' words are a channel of Satan's power.
The same set of implications attended Christian exorcisms after Jesus' death.
Controversy emerges at the very point where God's kingdom comes.

ISSUES

Who is really guilty of blasphemy—Jesus or the scribes?
Of the two groups, one serves Satan, one God; but both believe they serve God. Which group is deceived?
How does one distinguish the presence of God's kingdom from Satan's?
In a conflict between two authorities, one supported by the accepted religious leaders and the other rejected by those leaders, which should be preferred?

A POET SEES THE ISSUES

John Milton, *Paradise Lost*, book 3, lines 1–265.

48 Forgiveness or Blasphemy?

TEXT Jesus, to the paralytic: My son, your sins are forgiven.
The scribes: This is blasphemy. Who can forgive sins but God alone?
Jesus: In order that you may know that the Son of man has authority on earth to forgive sins . . . [to the paralytic] Stand up, take up your bed, and go home.

(Mark 2:5–7, 10–11)

SITUATION Mark 2:1–12; Luke 5:17–26; Matthew 9:1–8
The first major debate that led to the decision to destroy Jesus (Mark 3:6)

CONVICTIONS Jesus and the scribes accorded primacy both to God and to his authority.
Both considered sin a sin against God and therefore more serious than paralysis or other sickness.
They agreed that only God can forgive sins against God.
They agreed that unauthorized claims to forgive sin are blasphemy.
Jesus insisted that his claims were authorized.
The purpose of the cure: "that you may know"

IMPLICATIONS Forgiveness was a sign of the coming of God's kingdom.
It therefore offered ample reason to glorify God.
Jesus' whole mission was at stake: his identity as Son of man, his authority, his message to Israel, his offer of God's mercy in forgiveness, his power over paralysis.
This conflict anticipated the final conflict between Jesus and the scribes, and between God and Satan.

ISSUES Was Jesus authorized to forgive sin against God? The scribes said no; therefore this was blasphemy.
Their rejection separated them from the disciples and the crowd of believers.
How could such a shift of authority from heaven to earth be verified?
Was no third option possible? Could Jesus be neither blasphemer nor authorized agent of God?
When does the unexpected forgiveness of sin justify a new doctrine of God? When should an old doctrine result in a rejection of that forgiveness?

FURTHER REFLECTION Søren Kierkegaard, *Training in Christianity*, trans. Walter Lowrie (1941; paperback reprint, Princeton: Princeton University Press, 1944), pp. 12–34.

49   Creation—for Whom?

TEXT   God did not create us for the sabbath; he created the sabbath for us. (Mark 2:27)

SITUATION   Mark 2:23–28; Matthew 12:1–8; Luke 6:1–5; Hosea 6:6; Genesis 2:1–3; Deuteronomy 5:12–15

Debate between Jesus and the Pharisees over the disciples' infraction of the law governing the sabbath

CONVICTIONS   God is the creator both of man and the sabbath.

In creation, God gives priority to man over the sabbath, showing concern for meeting human needs.

God's desire for mercy, not sacrifice, is thus demonstrated.

The people of God should allow the same mercy and the same concern to determine their sabbath observance.

By their actions Jesus and his disciples exemplify God's will.

IMPLICATIONS   To adopt this precedent would in effect destroy the observance of the sabbath as a visible mark separating Israel from the Gentiles.

Jesus claims for himself and his disciples the same privileges accorded to David and the temple priests.

Jesus asserts that current behavior should be guided by the reality of God as a continuing creator rather than by God as a giver of the law.

Jesus acts as if he has authoritative knowledge of God's creative activity in the present. It is this knowledge that leads Jesus to the conviction that disciples have, in fact, been obeying God's intention in creating the sabbath.

ISSUES   Had Jesus been authorized and qualified to interpret the laws governing the sabbath?

Could Jesus and his disciples claim immunity to the penalties decreed by God for disobeying the Ten Commandments?

If one is free to abrogate this law on such self-centered grounds, does not the same freedom extend to all other laws?

If the same principle were applied to all of God's laws, would the result be social anarchy arising from giving priority to any fancied, transient sense of need?

FAITH VS. IDOLATRY   Martin Buber, "The Silent Question: On Henri Bergson and Simone Weil," in *The Writings of Martin Buber*, ed. Will Herberg (New York: Meridian Books, 1958), pp. 306–14.

50   You Hypocrites!

TEXT   Jesus, to the Pharisees and scribes: For the sake of your tradition, you have made void the word of God.

You hypocrites! It was about you that Isaiah prophesied when he said:

> "This people honors me with their lips,
> but their heart is far from me;
> in vain do they worship me,
> teaching as doctrines the precepts of men." (Matt. 15:6–9)

SITUATION   Matthew 15:1–20; Mark 7:1–23; Isaiah 29:13 (Septuagint)

Replying to their attack on his disciples, Jesus condemns the Pharisees and the scribes as worshiping God in vain.

CONVICTIONS   Both antagonists accept as God's word the commandment about parents.

By making their own precepts normative, the Pharisees have emptied God's Word of its authority.

Through Isaiah, God declares their worship false, their hearts far from God.

Deceiving themselves (hypocrites!), they have become God's enemies.

IMPLICATIONS   Worship, doctrine, and conduct—all are tested by the distance of hearts from God.

Theology and spiritual cardiology become inseparable, one the measure of the other.

Lip service or hypocrisy extends to many other matters: food, washing of pots, legal and liturgical rules, worship.

ISSUES   The issue between these adversaries cannot be resolved because there can be no objective measure of heart-distance from God.

Both sides are committed to a divine vocation in which any concession to the other spells disloyalty to God.

The debate involves more than individual disobedience; it determines the guidance of God's people by God's messengers.

Both sides appeal to the law and the prophets. On what basis can one appeal be preferred to the other?

THEOLOGY AS CRITICAL THEORY   Jürgen Moltmann, *The Crucified God: The Cross of Christ as the Foundation and Criticism of Christian Theology*, trans. R.A. Wilson and John Bowden (New York: Harper & Row, 1974), pp. 65–73.

51   You Weeds!

TEXT

The disciples: Do you know that the Pharisees were offended?
Jesus: Every plant which my heavenly Father has not planted will be rooted up.
(Matt. 15:12–13)

SITUATION

Matthew 15:12–14; 13:24–30; 23:29–33
Present: Pharisees, disciples, Jesus, crowds
Issue: What defiles a person?
Jesus addresses the disciples but deals with an issue raised by the Pharisees.

CONVICTIONS

God is Jesus' Heavenly Father, not the Father of opponents.
Jesus' Father plants seed with a view to harvesting a crop.
Another planter (Satan?) has planted other seed.
God will uproot those plants from his field (Israel?).
God limits defilement to what comes out of the heart.
Matthew sees this as applying to church leaders and their opponents, after Golgotha (15:20).

IMPLICATIONS

Every teacher of Israel belongs to one planting or the other.
Those whom Satan plants are blind guides (Matt. 15:14) who are concerned with avoiding external defilements.
Those whom God plants are teachers concerned only with internal defilements.
God authorizes those teachers to repudiate the whole body of laws concerning ritual impurity.
All foods, Jesus declares, are clean (Mark 7:19).

ISSUES

Whenever disciples confront opponents, the key question becomes, who planted whom—God or Satan?
Each group claims to teach God's Word, but one group empties that Word of its authority. Which group is this?
If Jesus and his representatives are allowed to cancel all scriptural regulations concerning purity, do they not become enemies of all religion?
Is there any way of avoiding this impasse between these two groups as interpreters of Scripture?

FOR REFLECTION

Martin Luther, *Lectures on Romans*, comments on Romans 2:22–29.

52   You Fools!

TEXT A Pharisee who asked him to dine was astonished to see that Jesus did not first wash before dinner.
Jesus: Now you Pharisees cleanse the outside of the cup . . . but inside you are full of greed and evil. You fools! Did not the Creator of the outside create the inside also? So give for alms those things that are inside. Then quickly everything will become clean for you.   (Luke 11:37-41)

SITUATION Luke 11:37–41
Debate at dinner; prelude to other denunciations of the Pharisees

CONVICTIONS God is the creator both of outside and of inside, i.e., the heart.
The heart is the source and location of all cleanness or uncleanness.
As God's creation, the heart is the nearest link to God, its creator.
By giving, the inside cleanses the outside; by seeking external cleansing, the heart becomes filthy.

IMPLICATIONS Jesus requires a revision of all perceptions—of sin, of self, of heart, of the law, of God. All this involves a new language about external and internal things.
As God's creation, one must give for alms the self that one has received from God—the self that is clean, the self that cleanses the outside.
Though God created both inside and outside, they are not equal. Inside purity is the source of outside purity, not vice versa.
This theology invalidates scriptural rules on how to purify oneself and makes fools of those who enforce these rules.

ISSUES At stake are attitudes toward God, creation, the Scriptures, the self, the function of religion, almsgiving, vocation, agelong tradition.
How are the unclean to be made clean? By obeying the scriptural rules of purity or by repenting of an unclean heart?
How could the Pharisees become clean except by renouncing their vocation and role in the synagogue?
Does the confrontation make clear why it was inevitable for these teachers to reject Jesus?

WHAT IS FAITH? Unamuno, *Tragic Sense of Life*, ch. 9 (first 8 pp.).

53　God Curses

TEXT

Jesus: Woe to you Pharisees! You tithe mint, rue, and every spice, and ignore the judgment and the love of God. You ought to have done these without neglecting the others. Woe to you Pharisees! You love the best seat in the synagogues and special greetings in the shopping malls. Woe to you! You are like graves that are unmarked, and people walk over them without knowing it. (Luke 11:42–44)

SITUATION

Luke 11:42–44; Matthew 23:23–27; Hebrews 10:1–10; Leviticus 24:30; Numbers 19:14–20

Jesus announces God's cursing of the Pharisees, in sharp contrast to his blessing of the disciples.

CONVICTIONS

Ignoring the Creator's judgment of "the inside" (text 52) leads to reliance on tithing the outside.

To seek the best seats is the kind of self-seeking the Creator detests.

Religious leaders who seek such honors become unmarked graves, the source of contamination.

God's approval is precluded by such social approval.

IMPLICATIONS

Jesus' announcement of God's curse is an implicit call to repent.

To repent is to remember that the inner self is God's creation.

The conflict—Jesus versus Pharisees—springs from two opposite conceptions of God's judgment and love.

Opposite also are the two ways of dealing with the conflict between inner motives and outer actions, between self-deception and truth.

ISSUES

The opposing conceptions of God's relation to the self makes religious conflict inescapable; this conflict becomes acute in proportion to the strength of loyalty to different gods.

An impasse develops between accredited specialists in biblical interpretation and an unaccredited prophet who claims to know both God's judgment and human hearts.

Differing conceptions of God and the self produce contradictory answers to the question, whom does God bless? and curse?

A PARALLEL TEXT

Søren Kierkegaard, *Attack upon "Christendom," 1854–1855*, trans. Walter Lowrie (Princeton: Princeton University Press, 1968), pp. 18–22.

54 God Detests

TEXT

Jesus: No one can be a slave to two lords. . . . You cannot act as a slave to both God and wealth.

The Pharisees were listening to these words and sneering at him.

Jesus: You show off your righteousness before others, but God knows your hearts. What human beings honor, that is what God detests.

(Luke 16:13–15)

SITUATION

Luke 16:13–15; Matthew 6:24; Proverbs 16:5

En route to Jerusalem, Jesus has been training the disciples; the Pharisees overhear and interrupt.

CONVICTIONS

It is an illusion of religious leaders to believe that God praises what they praise.

What they and others most covet is what God most detests;

God is revolted by what the Pharisees take to be proof of righteousness.

Just as the love of money excludes the love of Israel's God, so too the love of religious prestige is a form of slavery to wealth (another god).

Only God can discern these unconscious slaveries and unconfessed gods.

IMPLICATIONS

Slavery to God requires detesting what he detests.

Self-righteousness equals self-deception equals slavery to wealth.

Slavery to God requires total freedom from such slavery.

Jesus knew that this conflict would lead to violence (Luke 16:16).

His understanding of what God detests is needed even more by his disciples than by the Pharisees.

For a true knowledge of God, Pharisees are as dependent on Jesus as are his disciples.

ISSUES

Is this revelation of what God detests true?

Is it true that God initiated this attack on the Pharisees as an example of what God hates?

Is it true that this attack on what God detests was a factor leading to Jesus' death?

If this is true, did his death become a means of releasing the Pharisees from their slavery to self-deception?

BACKGROUND

Herman Melville, *Moby Dick* (New York: Random House, Modern Library, 1930), ch. 9.

55   God Is Happy

TEXT   The Pharisees: This man receives sinners and eats with them.
Jesus: There will be more joy in heaven over one sinner who repents than over ninety-nine righteous persons who need no repentance. (Luke 15:2,7)

SITUATION   Luke 15:1–32; Matthew 18:12–14
Three parables in Jesus' debate with Pharisees, as they protest his welcome to sinners
En route to Jerusalem

CONVICTIONS   God's action is compared to the actions of a shepherd, a housewife, a father.
God rejoices for and with each penitent sinner.
His joy explains why Jesus welcomes sinners and eats with them.
God ignores statistical measures of importance (one vs. ninety-nine).
Through Jesus, God carries out affirmative action for social and religious untouchables.
Joy creates an expanding solidarity in celebration:
God/Jesus/sinners/neighbors.

IMPLICATIONS   The three parables suggest the universal extension of God's love for the lost.
The role of the Pharisees emerges in the protests of the elder brother.
God authorizes and shares in the feasting, music, and dancing of the new family.
The only road to knowing this God and to sharing his joy is to be lost and to be found.
By their attitude toward sinners the Pharisees exclude themselves from that joy.

ISSUES   Is the picture of a joyful God intelligible? acceptable?
Is the picture of God's indifference to the ninety-nine acceptable?
What are the effects of this God-logic on religious institutions that rely on numbers, membership, status?
Does the parable anticipate the way in which the Passion story evoked similar anger and joy in synagogues and churches of the first century?
To be saved, must the Pharisees accept the definitions of life and death provided by the father in the parable?

BACKGROUND   Sobrino, *Christology at the Crossroads*, pp. 201–9.

56 Dinner Is Served!

TEXT
A king gave a marriage feast for his son, and sent his servants to call those who were invited.... They would not come.... They seized his servants ... and killed them. The king was angry ... and destroyed those murderers.... Go ... and invite to the marriage feast as many as you find. (Matt. 22:2–3, 6–7, 9)

SITUATION
Matthew 22:1–10; Luke 14:16–24
A parable told by Jesus against the scribes and Pharisees; an allegory in which the king equals God, his son equals Jesus, the servants equal Christian apostles and prophets, and those invited equal the Jewish leaders

CONVICTIONS
In fulfilling prophecy God has brought the kingdom near to Israel.
God has invited first those to whom the kingdom had been promised.
The leaders of God's people have refused the invitation and have rejected, even killed, the bearers of the invitation.
Invitations have been issued to others; they fill the hall and the tables.

IMPLICATIONS
Any blame for the change in wedding guests falls on the group invited first.
God includes within the kingdom only those who are worthy of it.
Worthiness is determined by response to God's messengers; no excuses are acceptable.
Inclusion in the wedding feast represents the highest reward.
Those included after the first selection need to be alert to meet continued requirements (Matt. 22:11–14).

ISSUES
Is Jesus the son of the king in the parable?
Are the messengers fully authorized to invite guests to dinner?
Can those invited believe that the dinner is ready?
Will God fulfill the threat of exclusion?
What kind of god sends troops to burn the city of those who spurn his invitation?

THINKING FURTHER
Paul Ricoeur, *Symbolism of Evil*, trans. Emerson Buchanan (Boston: Beacon Press, 1969), pp. 50–70.

57   A Haven for Prostitutes

TEXT   Prostitutes go into the kingdom of heaven before you. For John came to you along the path of righteousness, and you did not accept him but . . . the prostitutes accepted him. (Matt. 21:31–32)

SITUATION   Matthew 21:28–32; Luke 7:29, 30
A climactic debate in the temple. Jesus tells the chief priests and elders a parable that involves them in self-condemnation and that provokes them to try to arrest him.

CONVICTIONS   Jesus compares entrance into God's kingdom with a son's obedience to his father.
God refuses to confer such entrance on the religious leaders who rely on their good intentions.
These leaders have refused to accept God's demand for repentance and faith in John's announcement.
Instead, they have been alienated by God's acceptance of tax collectors and whores.
God's judgment coincides with their self-exclusion.

IMPLICATIONS   Jesus tells the parable to authorities who are supposed to hold the keys to the kingdom (Matt. 23:13).
The parable is designed to offend them, for tax-collectors are traitors to the nation and prostitutes break the Ten Commandments.
In God's view their action of repentance outweighs both the priests' standing and the sinners' wickedness.
The parable also implies that the exclusion of one group and the inclusion of the other vindicates God's justice and marks "the path of righteousness."

ISSUES   To whom has God given authority to determine who should be admitted to the kingdom?
What kind of community is this kingdom if it is a haven for traitors and whores and excludes all those with religious vocations?
If Israel is to be defined by those worthy to enter the kingdom, how does the parable redefine Israel?

IS THIS THE NEW CREATION?   Lionel S. Thornton, *The Dominion of Christ* (Westminster: Dacre Press, 1952), pp. 1–14.

58　A Stonemason

TEXT

The very stone which the builders rejected
　　　has become the head of the corner;
this was the Lord's doing,
　　　and it is marvelous in our eyes.　(Mark 12:10–11)

SITUATION

Mark 12:1–12; Matthew 21:33–46; Luke 20:9–19; Psalm 118:22–23
The conclusion of a parable told against priests, scribes, and elders
An interjection by believers, after the resurrection
The stone equals Jesus; builders equal scribes; Lord equals God; "our eyes"
　　　equals believers.

CONVICTIONS

God is like a vintner or a house builder, Israel like a vineyard or a house.
God has full rights to the harvest; God can install or evict tenants.
God has sent many rent collectors, all of whom have been rejected.
As the latest of these, Jesus has been sent to receive the rental due.
Rejection of Jesus means rejection of God's rights as owner.
God has rejected the rejecters; Jesus has been made the cornerstone.

IMPLICATIONS

God's care for the vineyard is constant: the vineyard remains; only the tenants
　　　are changed.
Installation of the cornerstone is a miracle of God's action.
Jesus' resurrection is interpreted as God's action in restoring the vineyard to
　　　faithful tenants.
In Mark's edition, the parable is a call to synagogue members to accept Jesus'
　　　messengers as their new leaders.
What has happened is to be understood in the light of Psalm 118.

ISSUES

Is this a valid interpretation of the psalm?
On what basis can Jesus claim to be God's collector of rents?
Is the rejection of Jesus as messenger a denial of God's will or obedience to it?
Must Israel now accept Gentiles as the new tenants?
Is Jesus' resurrection the only evidence that God acted to change the tenants in
　　　the vineyard?　How good is that evidence?

FUEL FOR THOUGHT

Pascal, *Pensées*, thoughts 606–19.

59   A Footstool

TEXT

Jesus: David himself, inspired by the Holy Spirit, declared,
    "The Lord [God] said to my Lord [the Messiah],
    Sit at my right hand
    until I put your enemies [leaders of Israel]
        under your feet."
David himself called him Lord; so how is he his son? (Mark 12:36–37)

SITUATION

Mark 12:35–37; Matthew 22:41–46; Luke 20:41–44; Psalm 110
One of the final debates in the temple before Jesus' arrest

CONVICTIONS

David was a prophet to whom God revealed the Messiah through the Spirit.
In fulfillment of his promise to David, God has placed Jesus on the throne of
    power.
This power was now being extended over Jesus' enemies.

IMPLICATIONS

Evangelists saw this happening in the period following the resurrection.
Scribal interpretations of prophecy and their expectations of the Messiah
    were false.
God's action explained both the hostility of the scribes and the joy of the
    crowds (vs. 37).
By identifying the Messiah, the resurrection of "my Lord" disclosed the
    meaning of all Jesus' earlier controversies with Israel's leaders.
In all those events God's intention had been to subject one-time enemies to
    the authority of Jesus.

ISSUES

Which is right—believers who accept the witness of David, Jesus, the Holy
    Spirit, and God or Israel's leaders, who reject that joint witness?
Are these opposing positions negotiable, or is there only one option: to reject
    Jesus or to be subjected to him?

THINKING THIS THROUGH

Søren Kierkegaard, "Has a Man the Right to Let Himself Be Put to Death for
the Truth?" in *The Present Age*, trans. Alexander Dru and Walter Lowrie
(London: Oxford University Press, 1940), pp. 86–99.

60   Trapping the Trappers

TEXT   Pharisees and Herodians: Is it lawful to pay tribute to the emperor or not?
Jesus: Pay to the emperor what is due the emperor; pay to God what is due God.
(Mark 12:14, 17)

SITUATION   Mark 12:13–17; Matthew 22:15–22; Luke 20:20–26; 23:2; John 19:15
Debate in Jerusalem with Pharisees and Herodians (Luke—scribes and chief
priests)
Adversaries are accused of malice (Matt.), craftiness (Luke), hypocrisy (Mark).
The Pharisees and Herodians are caught in their own clever trap.

CONVICTIONS   The answer forces the adversaries to decide which things are due God; this shifts
the issue from taxes to the authority, power, purpose, and gifts of God.
Thus they are forced to think about their own personal relationship to God (e.g.,
first commandment). Who is your god? Whose slave are you?

IMPLICATIONS   The Gospels assume that Jesus knew what belonged to God and that his
adversaries did not.
The stories that follow, especially the arrest and the trial, are designed to
disclose two antithetical answers to this riddle (e.g., John 19:12–15).
The context gives priority to "the things of God" (cf. "the way of God," vs. 14),
a priority that excludes allegiance to human rulers.

ISSUES   Is Jesus' answer anything more than an adept escape from the trap?
Does Jesus' response set a trap of his own?
Should a saying addressed to enemies be applicable without change to disciples?
Discussion of this story often evades the central question of what actually
belongs to God and what must therefore be treated as his.

RELEVANCE   H. Richard Niebuhr, "Toward the Independence of the Church," in Niebuhr,
William Pauck, and Francis P. Miller, *The Church Against the World* (Chicago:
Willet, Clark & Co., 1935), pp. 123–35.

61 What Power Is This?

TEXT

The Sadducees: In the resurrection whose wife will she be?
Jesus: You are wrong. . . . You know neither the scriptures nor the power of
God. . . . When they rise, they . . . are like angels in heaven. (Mark 12:23–25)

SITUATION

Mark 12:18–27; Matthew 22:23–33; Luke 20:27–40; Deuteronomy 25:5–10;
Genesis 38:8
A debate with the Sadducees over the resurrection, in which they present a
test case against the Pharisaic view

CONVICTIONS

God has power; God is the source of power.
Resurrection is a manifestation of this power.
Resurrection means becoming like angels in heaven (Luke, "sons of God,"
"sons of the resurrection"). The basic thought in these images is
presence with God and the sharing of God's life.
God's relation to the self is at a level deeper than the distinction between sexes;
a person's sex is a temporal feature; one's relation to God is eternal.

IMPLICATIONS

Before thinking resurrection, one should think God.
Before asking "What will I have?" ask "Whom do I serve?"
To focus attention on the husband-wife relationship is to restrict God's power
to the concern of the husband.
To be like angels is to share at least a double role: to worship and glorify God
and to serve as messengers to earth.
In relation to heaven, sex and marriage are matters limited to earthly existence.

ISSUES

Is this answer anything more than a nimble escape from a trap?
Is it a way of siding with the Pharisees against the Sadducees?
Or is it an example of two groups' (disciples and Sadducees) using the same
language but with different meanings?
Should all thinking about the future start with a recognition of the power of
God, the reality of heaven, the ignorance of creatures, the presumption of
wanting to know more than is possible about the future, the error in
making life with God an extension of earthly conditions?

A MEDITATION

Alan Paton, *Instrument of Thy Peace* (New York: Seabury Press, 1968), ch. 20
(pp. 111–18).

62   What Life Is This?

TEXT

Jesus: Have you not read in the book of Moses. . . . "I am the God of Abraham, and the God of Isaac, and the God of Jacob"? He is not God of the dead, but of the living. (Mark 12:26–27)

SITUATION

Mark 12:18–27; Matthew 22:23–33; Romans 14:7–9; Luke 20:27–40; John 5:19–29; Exodus 3:6

CONVICTIONS

Jesus illustrates the Sadducee's failure to understand the book of Moses.
God is alive as the eternal "I am."
He is therefore God of the living. "All live to him" (Luke 20:38).
The patriarchs share God's life, and Israel shares that life through them.
Jesus uses the book of Moses to speak to those present about living to and with the Eternal.

IMPLICATIONS

To know the Scriptures is to hear God speak through them now.
To know the power of God is to be in contact with God's life.
The deaths of Abraham, Isaac, and Jacob have not separated them from God's life.
Insofar as Israel shares their lives, death is not an end to this life. Such knowledge must change all thinking about life and death.
The adversaries use the same terms—death and life—but those terms carry very different meanings because of different understandings of God.

ISSUES

To what extent does this story indicate what it means to believe in the God of Jesus? the God of Israel?
Does this position help to separate Jesus' God-logic from that of the Pharisees and the Sadducees?
How did this conception of God's power contradict current conceptions of that power?
How did Jesus' faith in the God of the living condition early Christian thinking about resurrection, including Jesus' resurrection?

SOME LONG THOUGHTS

Pascal, *Pensées*, thoughts 184–94.

63 God Joins Together

TEXT

Pharisees: Is it lawful for a man to divorce his wife?

Jesus: From the beginning of creation, "God made them male and female." "For this reason a man will leave his father and mother and be joined to his wife, and the two will become one." So they are no longer two, but one flesh. What God has joined, let no one separate. (Mark 10:2, 6–9)

SITUATION

Mark 10:1–12; Matthew 19:1–12; Genesis 1:27; 2:24; Deuteronomy 24:1; 1 Corinthians 7:10–11

Debate with Pharisees in Judea

The two sides shared respect for Scripture as God's Word, but Jesus attacks their hardness of heart and their interpretation of Scripture.

CONVICTIONS

God created two sexes and joined them together.

God's purposes in creation should take precedence over Moses' purpose in law.

Jesus knew God's purposes both in creation and in marriage.

God's purposes in creation determine what happens in marriage.

The key question is not what is lawful, but what God intends and what he has done.

IMPLICATIONS

Two sides asked different questions of Scripture and received different answers about God.

Hardness of heart induced people to choose an easier course, in line with human desires rather than with what God has done.

Two sides adopted different ways of aligning human actions to God's purposes.

God's purpose was as difficult for the disciples to grasp and to obey as for the Pharisees (Matt. 19:10–12).

ISSUES

Which side was a better interpreter of Moses?

Which alternative took better account of human possibilities and institutional dynamics?

Did the two sides illustrate two opposing theologies that were mutually exclusive ways of thinking about God's creation and his action in such matters as marriage?

How far could either Pharisees or disciples go in allowing God's purpose in marriage to displace all human considerations?

AN EARLY CHRISTIAN VISION

1 Peter 3:1–12

64   God Retaliates

TEXT   Jesus: The Wisdom of God said "I will send them prophets and apostles, some of whom they will persecute and kill," that the blood of all the prophets, shed from the foundation of the world, may be required of this generation. (Luke 11:49–50)

SITUATION   Luke 11:45–51; Matthew 23:34–36; 2 Chronicles 24:20–22
Woes uttered against the lawyers (Matt., against the scribes and the Pharisees)

CONVICTIONS   God sends Christian prophets to Israel and its lawyers.
Those prophets have belonged to the line of messengers from the first.
The lawyers have belonged to the line of murderers, ever since Cain.
God holds this generation accountable for having shed the blood of all the
       prophets from the foundation of the world.
In sending messengers, God knows all this.

IMPLICATIONS   Jesus and his messengers belong to the line of God's prophets, which began with
       Abel.
Those who reject Jesus' messengers belong to the line of murderers, which
       began with Cain.
Jesus and his messengers have the key to knowledge that enables Israel to enter
       the kingdom of God.
The lawyers have taken away this key; they prevent others from entering the
       kingdom.

ISSUES   Is it true that God has drawn the line of division, not between synagogue and
       church, but between apostles and prophets on the one hand and scribes,
       Pharisees, and lawyers on the other?
Are they in fact responsible for the blood of all prophets?
Will God require that blood of them?

TWO CITIES AT WAR   Augustine, *The City of God*, part 3, book 1–3, chs. 1–6.

65   The Fatal "I Am"

TEXT

The High Priest: Are you the Christ, the Son of the Blessed?
Jesus: I am; and you will see the Son of man sitting at the right hand of power [Luke, "the power of God"] and coming with the clouds of heaven.
The High Priest: You have heard his blasphemy.
They all condemned him as deserving of death. (Mark 14:61–62, 64)

SITUATION

Mark 14:55–65; Matthew 26:59–68; Luke 22:66–71; Psalm 110:1; Daniel 7:13
A moment of truth: the hearing before the Sanhedrin
Jesus makes this declaration to the highest religious authority among his people.

CONVICTIONS

God has enthroned Jesus at his right hand, with power to execute God's government over Israel.
This enthronement fulfills at least two scriptural promises (Daniel and the Psalm).
It discloses as much about God as about Jesus.
The high priest, as representative of Israel, will "see" this manifestation of God's power.
Jesus' "I am" draws its full meaning from God's "I am," as an assertion of ultimate truth, authority, and life (Exod. 3:13–14).

IMPLICATIONS

The dramatic confrontation between Jesus and the high priest symbolizes the ultimate issue before Israel and determines the identity of the true Israel.
In this confrontation, both individuals are carrying out God's will, though the high priest does so unwittingly.
The scene presents the high priest as the official representative of Israel, but Jesus as the actual representative.

ISSUES

Is Jesus blaspheming God, or has God appointed Jesus to this hour?
Is the condemnation "deserving of death" true or false? by what criteria?
How does the text conceive of God's power? like or unlike the priest's power? like or unlike Jesus' power at that moment?
Does the reference to God's power call for the high priest to redefine such words as power/weakness, glory/shame, defeat/victory?

ON THE DEATH OF GOD

Eugene Rosenstock-Huessy, *The Christian Future* (New York: Harper & Row, 1966), pp. 92–102.

66 The Final Silence

TEXT Chief priests and scribes: He saved others; he cannot save himself. Let the Christ, the King of Israel, come down from the cross, that we may see and believe.
Jesus: [silence . . . no reply] (Mark 15:31–32)

SITUATION Mark 15:22–32; Matthew 27:33–44; Luke 23:33–38
The crucifixion
Mocking by the religious authorities, followed by the silence of Jesus

CONVICTIONS Here Jesus is speaking through his silent presence on the cross.
He is speaking as God's anointed and as Israel's king.
It is God's will that Jesus should save others by not being able to save himself.
That very inability discloses God's way of saving others; it indicates the kind of power this weakness exerts.
To "see and believe" is to see and believe this about God.

IMPLICATIONS In an ironical way, the Gospels accept as true the accusation "he cannot save himself."
The scene makes clear the radically different conceptions of salvation, kingship, the cross, blasphemy, faith, Israel.
The text rejects any theology that says in effect, "He trusts in God; therefore God should deliver him" (Matt. 27:43).
It also rejects any theology that says of this scene, "If God is good, he is not here."
The scoffers express a view of God that was held on that occasion by everyone but Jesus.

ISSUES Which is God—the god of the high priest or the god of Jesus?
Both agree that salvation is salvation from death; they disagree on which death is the true death.
The mocking versus the silence poses a true-false question that epitomizes the entire story of Jesus.
Is the plea of the priests—"that we may see"—linked to the promise of Jesus—"and you will see" (Mark 14:62)?

BACKGROUND Psalm 22

One God or Two?

Having surveyed more than twenty texts in which Jesus addressed his opponents, we should be able to assess the issues that divided them. Before doing this, however, we should review the evidence provided in the earlier section (texts 1–42), in which Jesus instructed his followers by using his adversaries as a foil for his teachings. These opponents were "the wise and understanding," from whom the knowledge of the Father and the Son had been hidden. They were the wolves among whom the helpless lambs had been sent. They ruled the synagogue, where disciples were forced either to confess or to deny faith in Christ. They were the persecutors whom disciples were forbidden to fear. They were offended by the company Jesus had chosen to keep; he, in turn, was offended by their refusal to join that company. Sometimes they initiated the charge that he was in collusion with Satan; at other times he initiated the same charge against them. To him, their reliance on oaths, like many of their interpretations of Scripture, originated with the Evil One. They claimed honorific titles, prestigious places, and special privileges, all of which his disciples must renounce. Their punctilious observance of such duties as almsgiving, prayer, and fasting were hypocritical masks for their craving of public praise, canceling any possibility of praise from God. In the language of the parable, "they trusted in themselves that they were righteous and despised others" (Luke 18:9).

To the Evangelists all this was true. Even so, they held to the knowledge that God continued to send rain and sun upon these very opponents. They were enemies whom God loved and for whom disciples must pray. Only by being merciful to them could disciples count upon God's mercy. From the scribes these disciples had inherited "Moses' seat," though this inheritance required totally different practices (Matt. 23:2–3). Jesus' crucifixion at enemy hands must be accepted as an essential feature of the disciples' mission to Israel. The picture is grim but remarkably consistent.

The dark lines become even more deeply etched when data from section 2 is added. Here the evidence must seem very surprising to many modern readers. A first surprise is the extent and depth of the enmity. The confrontations began at the very start of Jesus' ministry (Mark 3:6; Matt. 5:10; Luke 4:29). Throughout that ministry the plotting continued until it reached explosive intensity in the trial and its inevitable verdict. Many Gospel stories read like dispatches from battlefields in a seemingly nonnegotiable war.

A second surprise for many readers is the discovery of how frequently the Gospels cast Jesus in the role of an aggressor. He brought a sword rather than peace. On many occasions he took the initiative in attacking the establishment, claiming that such attacks had been authorized and even commanded by his Commissioner. To be sure, on occasion his enemies took the initiative; but in most cases the Evangelists presented their actions as a counterattack, not merely against Jesus but against God. Whether they were attacks or counterattacks, the confrontations were seen as inescapable instances of God's controversy with his people. Such, at least, is a basic conviction of all four Gospels.

And there is a further conviction: that these earthly controversies should be traced to invisible sources, to the heavenly warfare between God and Satan. In the debates over the law, for example, invisible heavenly powers were contending for the loyalty of Israel and of every Israelite. If Israel had become "an evil and adulterous generation," it was only because Israel had been deceived and seduced by the devil. The mission of Jesus was God's strategy for bringing the people to repentance. At first that strategy worked better with the helpless and the outcasts than with their leaders. To reach the latter, God's anointed must take the struggle into their stronghold, where their authority was unchallenged—into the synagogue and the temple. It was there that the struggle would reach its climax and its resolution.

The altercations were intense enough on the human level, but seen as instances of cosmic warfare they became even more vigorous and violent. This hidden background produced a sense of inevitability: "the Son of man must die." At first, of course, the disciples refused to accept this necessity, but Jesus seems never to have doubted it. In the Passion story in each Gospel, the fateful conflict is seen, not simply as an index of the blindness of Jesus' enemies and Jesus' own fidelity, but as an index of God's inflexibility and Satan's resourcefulness. This inevitability makes the Gospel stories relevant to the story of Israel from beginning to end, and even to the story of God's creation since Cain and Abel.

One thing is strangely absent from these stories of deadly conflict. We do not find theologians debating directly which ideas of God are true or false or which doctrines must be defended or attacked. It is not easy to point to any text in which the issue under debate is a formal doctrine about God or God's attributes. This absence has led many interpreters to suppose that Jesus and his enemies shared one and the same God. For example, a highly respected scholar has written:

> In the N.T. there is not—nor in the nature of things can there be—any original doctrine of God, for the God of whom Jesus and the apostles speak is none other than the God known by all the people, the God of the old covenant, the one, living, jealous and merciful God, the holy God to whom men owe obedience and loyalty.
> (R. Mehl, "God: N.T.," in J.-J. Von Allmen, *Vocabulary of the Bible* [London: Lutterworth Press, 1958], p. 146)

Rather, in the texts we have studied, the conflicts between Jesus and his adversaries were almost always rooted in their diverse thinking about God. In many cases it was Jesus' understanding of the God of Israel that aroused opposition from the leaders of Israel. Formal doctrines may have been absent, but the deepest conflicts stemmed from opposing perceptions of how God chooses to be present and active.

If these divergent views of God had not been supported by the strongest kind of vocational loyalties on both sides, their defenders would not have confronted one another as murderers and martyrs. If we hold that they were one in their views of God, we must concede that the operative inferences from that theology were diametrically opposed. The character of the religious dynamics is recognized in the Gospel of John:

They will put you out of the synagogues; indeed, the hour is coming when whoever kills you will think he is offering service to God. And they will do this because they have not known the Father, nor me. (16:2–3)

Each side considered itself loyal to the God of Israel, but the life-and-death struggle demonstrated the hidden activity of two gods. The issue, then, is this: which of these gods is the God of Abraham, Isaac, and Jacob? Which of the two groups of loyalists has been deceived into becoming children of Satan?

In the grammar of the Gospels, then, God's war with Satan in heaven entailed a showdown on earth between Jesus and his enemies. That struggle placed at stake all human knowledge of the heavenly antagonists. The climax and resolution of the struggle came with the crucifixion. That was the event in which God showed most clearly that he detested what the rulers of Israel prized. It was there that the prophecy of the high priest was fulfilled: "It is more expedient for you that one man should die for the people, and that the whole people should not perish" (John 11:50). That was precisely God's view also, though the high priest's understanding of it was false. The death of this one man meant life for the people.

A survey of these texts makes abundantly clear how difficult it would have been for the high priest to have recognized the presence of God in the crucified Jesus. Jean Milet's judgment on this matter is supported by virtually every point at issue between Caiaphas and the Evangelists.

> For a pious Jew, an assiduous temple worshiper, a scrupulous observer of the law, to be able to put his faith in such a new 'representation' of the deity required more than a change of mind; it called for a kind of 'delirious' abandonment of all the norms to which mind and heart had hitherto been subjected. . . . A mental effort of such magnitude was an unparalleled demand on a human being. . . .[Such Jews] were being asked to trample underfoot their most sacred convictions, to transform 'sacrilege' into a mystery of faith.
>
> (Jean Milet, *God or Christ: The Excesses of Christocentricity* [New York: Crossroad, 1981] pp. 17, 18)

Perceptive readers will have observed the absence from this group of texts of a twin metaphor that dominated the earlier group. As noted in the first section in Jesus' dialogues with his disciples the most frequent metaphor for God was Father. In this section we note that in his debate with his adversaries, Jesus never used that metaphor or its twin, sons. This is awesome evidence that we are dealing with two separate worlds and with language systems that are indigenous to those two worlds. Though they used the same vocabulary, disciples and adversaries belonged to two different metaphorical universes, to two different theologies. As Jon Sobrino has said:

> Jesus was condemned for blasphemy, not for heresy. Thus his conception of God was not only different from, but radically opposed to, that held by the established religion. (*Christology at the Crossroads*, p. 367)

One key to the apostolic awareness of this chasm is the care with which early Christian writers frequently referred to their deity in the phrase "*the* God *and* Father of our Lord Jesus Christ." (Rom. 1:7; 15:6; 1 Cor. 1:3; 8:6; 15:24; 2 Cor. 1:3; 6:8; 11:31; Gal. 1:1–4; Eph. 1:3; 6:23; Phil. 1:2; 4:20; James 1:27; 3:9; 1 Peter 1:3; John 8:19, 41; 20:17; Rev. 1:6). Paul's statement is typical:

Indeed there are many gods and many lords, yet for us there is one God, the Father . . . and one Lord, Jesus Christ. (1 Cor. 8:6)

In this connection I cite again the story of Jesus' trial before the high priest. At that final meeting between the most revered representative of Israel and the challenger, the carefully phrased question "are you . . . the Son of the Blessed?" elicited the direct answer: "I am" (text 65). That answer was followed by the explosive ejaculation, "Blasphemy." It should be clear that the high priest's revulsion was due as much to his prior conception of "the Blessed" as to his view of Jesus. His god could not conceivably be the father of such a son. It is in recognition of that impossibility that the Evangelists had reported that "no one knows . . . who the Father is except the Son and anyone to whom the Son chooses to reveal him." (text 4). According to all the Gospels, it was as a revealer of this Father that Jesus was crucified.

JESUS
AND
THE UNSEEN WORLD

JESUS
AND
THE UNSEEN WORLD

It is on the basis of Christ that we know who God is and what it means to be a human being. God is not just any deity: God is first and foremost the Father of Jesus. To be a human being is not simply to possess the essence of a rational animal; it is to be like Jesus.

—Sobrino, *Christology at the Crossroads* (pp. 329–30)

The Gospels narrate stories of intense conflict, a warfare that the narrators believed to have had both primal and eschatological dimensions. These dimensions inhered in the conviction that the ultimate antagonists were God and Satan. This feature invests with special significance the reports of Jesus' conversations with Satan and God. We encounter only a few of these conversations, but those few are decisive.

Be aware of the difficulties that the narrators faced in reporting such conversations. Usually, if not always, the dialogues took place when no other human beings were at hand to watch or to eavesdrop. Thus the narrators were forced to venture into areas often regarded as off-limits to third parties. In telling what happened, they were implicitly compelled to claim a kind of literary omniscience. They not only had to ignore their distance in space and time from the original conversations but also had to invade with journalistic brashness the psychic privacy of the person of Jesus. Some of these difficulties were overcome by the conviction that what transpired in the secret dialogues explained the visible conflicts between Jesus and his known adversaries. Because the narrators knew the course and the outcome of those conflicts, they could reconstruct the hidden origins. They could guard against undue presumption by surrounding the scene with an appropriate sense of the mystery that surrounds all human discourse with the Divine or the demonic. Success or failure in telling what Jesus and his unseen interlocutors said or did would be measured by the degree of coherence between the unknown and the known.

In telling stories of Jesus' conversation with Satan or God, then, the narrators assumed certain things. For instance, they assumed that each conversation was decisive in determining later developments in the public realm. This assumption, in turn, invested the words of the conversations with highly symbolic overtones; Jesus' words conveyed the inner meaning not only of the particular episode but also of the story of his mission from beginning to end. His words, in fact, interpreted God's purposes in sending him on this assignment. Accordingly, Jesus' dialogues with Satan and with God not only were consistent with the rest of the Gospel story but provided the redemptive meaning of Jesus' dialogues — with friends and foes alike — which were in the public domain. Because narrators compiled the stories in this way, we should understand them against this background. Read the accounts of Jesus' conversations with God or Satan against the background of the other texts surveyed. How does each conversation disclose the origins and the dynamics of the drama as a whole? Which of the unseen actors in the story was finally defeated? or victorious?

Because it is in this way that I approach these ten texts, the comments will be arranged under two main headings: the inferences that may legitimately be drawn from each text and the linkages that exist in the Gospels between that text and the other texts that have been examined. Here, as in the earlier sections, attention will be focused upon attitudes toward God and toward God's archrival, Satan.

These stories articulate a way of detecting and defeating false expectations concerning the Deity, expectations common among the earliest Christian readers of the Gospels. It was customary for those readers, like their successors, to suppose that God, if truly God, would offer protection from danger or grant them some kind of immunity. The thrust of all these texts was to refute this expectation, this implicit theology, not only in order to show its falsity but also to trace its origin to Satan and to identify those who entertained it as unwitting servants of Satan. Accordingly, in telling these stories, the Evangelists had in mind very important theological objectives. Every misconception of the mission of the Son of God revealed demonic misconceptions of the purposes of his Father.

Four texts are located at the beginning of Jesus' work; they articulate the struggle between God and Satan as each sought to win Jesus' undivided allegiance. Three texts come from the course of Jesus' ministry; they disclose how that same struggle informed Jesus' efforts to train his disciples. Three texts are from the end of the story; these suggest how God was both present and absent when the final decisions were being made. Indirectly all ten texts reveal what it means for human beings to be slaves to these two competing lords and what it means to be lords of such slaves. Indirectly the texts also confirm earlier findings about the two opposing worlds and the languages indigenous to those worlds.

TEXTS

67. A Dove Descends

68. A Survival Kit

69. Who Is Testing Whom?

70. The Gift of Kingdoms

71. A Trap

72. A Treasure Hunt

73. A Cupful

74. The Forsaken Son

75. The Forgiven Enemies

76. The Father's Hands

Tests of Sonship

67 A Dove Descends

TEXT

Jesus was baptized by John. . . . He saw the heavens opened and the Spirit descending upon him like a dove; and a voice came from heaven: "You are my Son, my beloved. I am well pleased with you." (Mark 1:9–11)

SITUATION

Mark 1:1–11; Matthew 3:13–17; Luke 3:21–22; Mark 10:35–45; 11:30; Luke 12:50; Acts 10:36–38

The beginning of the Gospel in the baptism by John

In Mark, God's voice is addressed to Jesus, not to anyone else.

INFERENCES

God was the first to disclose the identity of Jesus as his Son and therefore of himself as Jesus' Father.

God chose the act of repentance in baptism as a place and a time most appropriate for such a disclosure.

One variant text—"today I have begotten you"—stressed the importance of repentance.

The descent of the Spirit qualified Jesus as Son to represent the Father in speech and action.

The description of this event was reminiscent of the visions and auditions that had been experienced by prophets both in Old and in New Testaments.

All later Gospel texts presupposed the actuality of God's choice of Jesus as God's Son.

LINKAGES

Jesus saw this initial event as something to be completed in his martyrdom (Mark 10:35–45).

The apostles typically associated the birth of their converts as God's children with their baptism.

Jesus' baptism clarified the meanings conveyed by the call for repentance and by the promise of forgiveness of sins (Mark 1:4).

Matthew and Luke introduced into the scene at the Jordan the future enemies of John and Jesus (Matt. 3:7–10, Luke 3:7–9).

The Risen Lord commanded his apostles to baptize believers.

DID GOD PLACE JESUS ON TRIAL?

Sobrino, *Christology at the Crossroads*, pp. 95–102.

68　A Survival Kit

TEXT　　The devil: If you are the Son of God, command these stones to become loaves of bread.
Jesus: It is written: man shall not live by bread alone, but by every word that proceeds from the mouth of God. (Matt. 4:3–4)

SITUATION　　Matthew 4:1–4; Luke 4:1–4; Deuteronomy 8:1–6
Those involved: Jesus, the Holy Spirit, the devil, angels.
An immediate sequel to baptism; the first indication of Jesus' guidance by the Holy Spirit (Matt. 3:17)
An immediate prelude to ministry, qualifying Jesus to exorcise demons and to free the devil's captives

INFERENCES　　Baptism introduces a person to the war between God and Satan.
That war tests the power of God's Word (command, promise).
Satan: A son is entitled to use God's Word as a means of survival.
Jesus: God's Word must not be used for selfish gain.
Satan defines life by what is sustained by bread.
Jesus defines life by reliance on God's Word.
Satan defines sonship by special privilege.
Jesus rejects Satan's appeal to his special status with a rule applied to all.
Jesus reads Deuteronomy 8:1–6 as God's use of manna to test Israel's willingness to depend on God alone.
God is pictured as speaker of a Word that sustains life for those who are humbled by it, who are content to be tested by it, who are so dependent on it that it displaces the desire for survival—the desire that is Satan's basic weapon.

LINKAGES　　To the calls to disciples to leave all and to the requirement that they take up their crosses
To the texts that define fatherhood and sonship
To the prohibitions of anxiety about food and to the assurances of God's care for sparrows
To the texts demonstrating Jesus' authority over demons
To the texts that stress the presence of the Holy Spirit in time of trial
To texts illustrating contrasts between two types of power, between two perceptions of the omnipotence of God
To the prayer for bread in Matthew 6:11

A LATER ANALOGY?　　T.S. Eliot, *Murder in the Cathedral* (New York: Harcourt, Brace, 1935), pp. 23–46; also in *The Complete Poems and Plays, 1909–1950* (New York: Harcourt, Brace & World, 1962), pp. 183–97.

69 Who Is Testing Whom?

TEXT   The devil, on the pinnacle of the temple: If you are the
Son of God, throw yourself down; for it is written:
> "He will give his angels charge of you"

and
> "On their hands they will bear you up,
> lest you strike your foot against a stone."

Jesus: It is also written: "You shall not put the Lord your
God to the test." (Matt. 4:5–7)

SITUATION   Matthew 4:5–7; Luke 4:9–12; Psalm 91:11–12; Deuteronomy 6:16–19;
Exodus 17:1–7
The same as Text 68.

INFERENCES   Here the Messiah was put to the test by the devil, but also by the Spirit, hence,
by God. Satan tested Jesus to see whether he would put God to the test.
God's Word is not to be used to secure immunity to danger or death. Rather,
it calls to greater danger and certain death. This raises the question of
when death is actually death.
Jesus could act as God's Son only by refusing immunity; this reflected two
conflicting definitions of sonship.
By his false idea of sonship, Satan disclosed a false idea of fatherhood.
By passing his test (with his convictions concerning survival, life, death,
sonship) Jesus helped others pass similar tests: like Son, like other sons.
By his victory, Jesus reversed the failures of Israel in the wilderness at
Massah (Deut. 6:16–19; Exod. 17:1–7).

LINKAGES   To stories of Gethsemane and Calvary: "He saved others; he cannot save
himself"
To the first commandment
To demands for an undivided heart
To other stories of Jesus in the temple, including his cleansing of it
To the activity of angels as God's messengers (Note their place in Satan's
world [Matt. 4:6] and in God's [vs. 11].)

ANOTHER MAN'S
STRUGGLE WITH SATAN   Morris West, *Proteus* (New York: William Morrow, 1979), pp. 292–324.

70 The Gift of Kingdoms

TEXT   Satan and Jesus on a high mountain, viewing all the kingdoms of the world and their glory.

Satan: All these I will give you, if you fall down and worship me.

Jesus: Be gone, Satan. For it is written, "You shall worship the Lord your God, and him only shall you serve." (Matt. 4:8–10)

SITUATION   Matthew 4:8–10; Luke 4:5–8; Deuteronomy 6:16

Transition from wilderness to temple to mountain indicates relevance to all places. The nature of each test dictates a suitable locale.

INFERENCES   God requires his Son to reject Satan's definitions of power, glory, and kingdom.

There are two kinds of worship. The worship of Jesus' God excludes seeking these goals.

Jesus' God is not to be found in the arena of the "kingdoms of the world" or in the history of those kingdoms.

Satan's test assumes a universal human desire for power and glory; it assumes that people naturally think of God as one who grants such gifts.

Jesus' knowledge of God and his worship enables him to penetrate Satan's deceptions.

LINKAGES   To all uses of the twin metaphor king/kingdom as applied to God and Jesus

To all texts referring to God's kingdom, power, glory

To the first commandment as the key to worship

To texts dealing with the heart as the place for the conjunction of the will of the Lord and that of his slaves

To God's gift of his kingdom to the "little flock"

To other dialogues in which the issue is what God can or cannot do

A SAINT'S FINAL PRAYER   Bernanos, *Star of Satan*, pp. 343–48.

71   A Trap

TEXT

Jesus began to show his disciples that he must suffer many things from the elders and chief priests and scribes.

Peter, rebuking him: God forbid, Lord. This shall never happen to you.

Jesus: Be gone, Satan. You are placing a stumbling block in my path. Your concern is not with God's goals, but with human goals. (Matt. 16:21–23)

SITUATION

Matthew 16:21–23; Mark 8:31–33; Luke 9:22
The conversation with Satan is an inset within the conversation with Peter.

INFERENCES

Satan disguises his appeal to self-interest by stressing the importance of Jesus in God's work.

The conflict between Satan and God grows out of two mentalities and two logics with regard to the rejection, suffering, and death of God's Son and sons.

The conversation implies that Peter's words are Satan's and that Jesus' words are God's.

Satan's logic has succeeded with elders, with chief priests, and with Peter. It threatens to succeed with Jesus and therefore with all Christians.

By identifying Satan, by spotting his trap, Jesus' victory becomes God's victory; it verifies Jesus' authority as God's anointed one (Matt. 16:16).

LINKAGES

Three Gospels see this story as an anticipation and an epitome of the Passion story, with its disclosure of divine, satanic, and human points of view.

The Gospels see this choice as defining the meaning of sonship and discipleship, each follower being susceptible to the same confusion as Peter's.

The Gospels see the struggle between Jesus and his disciples as instances of the war between God and Satan.

This text links the initial testing to Satan's testing of Jesus at midcourse and at the end of his work.

HELP IN IDENTIFYING SATAN

W. H. Auden, "New Year Letter, Part II," in *The Collected Poetry of W. H. Auden* (New York: Random House, 1945), pp. 274–90.

72   A Treasure Hunt

TEXT

Jesus, rejoicing in the Holy Spirit:

I thank you, Father, Lord of heaven and earth,
that you have hidden these things from the wise and understanding,
and have revealed them to babes.
Yes, Father, for such was your gracious will. (Luke 10:21)

SITUATION

Luke 10:17–24; Matthew 11:20–30; 1 Corinthians 1:26–31
A prayer or hymn of praise, possibly used in church
Jesus' response to both hostility (Matt.) and success (Luke)
"The wise" refers to unrepentant Israel; "babes" refers to repentant Israel, the
    infant children of God.

INFERENCES

God is Lord of heaven and earth.
God is recognized as Father, whose will is gracious.
God's grace is at work in both hiding and disclosing that will.
God makes the greatest treasure known to the least deserving.
Knowledge of the source of "these things" marks the boundaries between two
    communities.
This knowledge anticipates two destinies: hades or heaven.
Doxologies are expressions of joy in the Holy Spirit on the part of Jesus, his
    disciples, the babes.
This joy, this gratitude, is itself a gift of God and a share in his joy.

LINKAGES

To all texts that mention the last, the least, the lost
To all texts that reflect this bond defining sonship/fatherhood
To all texts that stress the initiative of God, whose action of hiding and
    disclosing is correlated with human responses of repentance or hostility
The prayer covers the whole story of the Gospels and the internal and external
    life of the early church.
The prayer traces the origin of the two languages (that of the wise and that of the
    babes) to God's choice of speaking in these terms.
The two languages refer not only to the conflicts between the wise and babes but
    also to the inner conflicts within each babe.

CONFESSION OF A BABE   Dumitriu, *Incognito*, pp. 348–59.

73   A Cupful

TEXT

Jesus: Abba, Father, all things are possible to you; remove this cup from me. Yet not what I will, but what you will. (Mark 14:36)

SITUATION

Mark 14:32–42; Matthew 26:36–46; Luke 22:40–46; John 12:27–33; Hebrews 10:1–10

Prayer in Gethsemane, immediately before the arrest

Cup means "the hour" (Mark 14:41) of denial, betrayal, shame, rejection, death.

INFERENCES

Though invisible, God is closer to Jesus than the disciples are.

As Father, God has placed this cup before Jesus. He can also remove it.

As Father, he has failed to remove it; so God wills Jesus' death.

The coincidence of the two wills, after a struggle between them, discloses the actuality of fatherhood/sonship.

The two wills might be viewed as situated wholly within the heart of Jesus.

The story raises the questions, does the offering of the cup prove or disprove God's fatherhood? Jesus' sonship?

LINKAGES

To all other texts dealing with the testing of Jesus and of the disciples

To all other texts presenting the command to "watch" (Mark 13:37)

To the character of prayer for the disciples

To the prayer, in Mark, from the cross (cf. text 74)

To the meanings intrinsic to baptism and the Last Supper

To the references to Jesus as the one sent from and by the Father

To Jesus' predictions that the Son of man must suffer, hence to other texts indicating that God wills the suffering of disciples.

A MUSICAL INTERPRETATION OF GETHSEMANE

Johann Sebastian Bach, *The Passion According to Matthew*, movements 24–32.

74   The Forsaken Son

TEXT   Jesus: My God, my God, why have you forsaken me? (Mark 15:34)

SITUATION   Mark 15:22–37; Matthew 27:45–50; Psalm 22; Malachi 4:5
In Mark and Matthew, these are the only words uttered on the cross.
The listeners' misunderstanding of the words implies linkage to Elijah, who was
      expected to return as herald of God's kingdom.
The words were accompanied by darkness over the land.

INFERENCES   God did forsake Jesus, at least in one sense. To be forsaken by God is assumed
      to be a measure of greatest agony and dereliction.
For Jesus to pray to God also implies that God was present to him even then.
The quotation from Psalm 22 implies that Jesus' God is the God of the psalmist
      and that his trust in God is like that of the psalmist.
The misunderstanding of Jesus' words (Mark 15:35) suggests that Jesus'
      dialogue with his Father was something that bystanders could not
      understand.
The Evangelists assumed that the answer to "Why?" involved God's desire to
      save both his disciples and his enemies.

LINKAGES   The forsakenness of this martyr indicates God's solidarity with the helpless, the
      ostracized, the poor, the babes, the martyrs.
This text is similar to other texts that stress God's fatherhood of children even
      when these children seem to suffer total loss.
The confession of the centurion (Mark 15:39) is an essential part of the same
      story, as is the tearing of the temple curtain.
To the Evangelists this cry is wholly consistent with the accounts of Jesus'
      testing after his baptism.
The scene as a whole is intended by both Mark and Matthew as a demonstration
      of Jesus' kingship, his sonship, and his role as Savior (Mark 15:31–32).

ABSENT OR PRESENT?   Samuel Terrien, *The Elusive Presence: Toward a New Biblical Theology* (1978:
paperback reprint, New York: Harper & Row, 1983), pp. 473–75.

75 The Forgiven Enemies

TEXT Father, forgive them, for they do not know what they are doing. (Luke 23:34)

SITUATION Luke 23:26–34
In Luke the first word from the cross
Them and *they* refer to the crucifying soldiers.

INFERENCES The Father has the power to forgive enemies; "only God can forgive sin"
(Mark 2:7).
Only God and Jesus know what the soldiers are actually doing.
The Father will honor the Son's request because their wills have become one.
The grace of one has become the grace of the other.
For Luke the words articulate the power of the cross in God's forgiveness of
his enemies, proving that the power of God is greater than that of his
enemies.
Even so, the daughters of Jerusalem have full occasion to weep (vs. 28).
Of those present, only the Father and the Son know what is transpiring,
though the Evangelists trust that their readers will understand.

LINKAGES To the Lord's Prayer for the disciples
To all texts that spell out the interdependence of Father and Son and to the
texts that define how sons act as sons
To all teachings that define the duties of sons to pray for their persecutors
To texts stressing the reversals in meaning of such terms as life, death, great,
small, shame, glory, first, last, weakness, power
To the text that asserts that only this Son can reveal his Father, and this Father
his Son

THE POWER OF FORGIVENESS Laurens van der Post, *The Prisoner and the Bomb* (New York: William
Morrow, 1971), pp. 66–74, 131–36.

76   The Father's Hands

TEXT   Father, into your hands I entrust my spirit. (Luke 23:46)

SITUATION   Luke 23:44–46; Psalm 31:5
In Luke Jesus' last words on the cross
The utterance coincides with the darkening of the sun and the tearing of the temple curtain, with the moment of death, and with the centurion's confession.
"A loud voice" is a mark of eschatological finality and cosmic range.
"[God's] hands" indicate the place of ultimate security.

INFERENCES   God as Father is source and home of Jesus' "spirit."
The Psalm quoted speaks of God as rock, refuge, fortress, guide, redeemer. "Take me out of the net which is hidden for me" (Psalm 31:4).
This trust marks the eternal unity of Father and Son.
This account of the final testing of Jesus matches the account of his first test (Luke 4:1–13).
Jesus' death is climactic evidence of his sonship and of God's fatherhood, inducing the centurion to praise God and the multitude of Jews to beat their breasts (Luke 23:47–48).

LINKAGES   The prayer may be intended to recall the gift of the Spirit in baptism.
The citing of this psalm recalls other Scriptures to which Jesus referred when an understanding of his work was at stake.
The story is taken as verification that throughout the Gospel story the will of God as Father was identified with the will of Jesus as Son.
The story is assumed to be a paradigm for the witness, work, and martyrdom of Jesus' disciples.
This word concerning the Spirit may be connected in Luke's mind to the promise of the Spirit, which will enable the disciples to take up their work (Acts 1:8; 2:4).

ABSENT OR PRESENT   Acts 7:51–60

Tests of Sonship

The texts reviewed in this section arouse both embarrassment and bafflement among many modern readers—embarrassment because in our world of thought such conversations with Satan and God seem unnatural and forced, bafflement because we do not know quite what to do with such conversations. To dismiss the stories out of hand leaves a bad conscience, for these were obviously of key importance to the Evangelists. Yet it is impossible to assign them similar importance in our own situation. The distance between our minds and those of the Evangelists is nowhere more obvious; the Evangelists show no signs of embarrassment. We are more at home in reporting ordinary conversations between two human beings; they seem more at home in reporting conversations with the unseen world. We require translation of their language into a more familiar human idiom in order to make it intelligible. Yet such translation often destroys the original substance and resonance.

What can be done to reduce our bafflement without demeaning the Evangelists' thought? For one thing, we can read each of these texts as an intended epitome of Jesus' whole ministry. As such, the texts have an advantage over more specific conversations that must be limited to a given place and a given moment. Each dialogue with the unseen world discloses what was happening at many places and times. Each expresses Jesus' hidden but profound dependence on his Father and his inner victories over Satan. By disclosing the activity of both God and Satan within the strategic struggles of Jesus' heart, the stories disclose the undivided loyalty of that heart. Had his heart been immune to such a struggle, the accounts of testing would have been useless. It was the reality of the struggle that demonstrated how two wills, the will of the Father and his own, had become fused in his heart. The intimacy of the Gospel reports bespeaks the reality of that fusion. These reports provide excellent definitions of personal obedience to the first commandment, and therefore excellent illustrations of the twin metaphor father/son. But a comprehension of that deeper level of reality would have been impossible apart from the conflict between God and Satan related in these narratives.

Another road toward comprehension is to note how the struggle focused on appeals to Scripture. The testing of Jesus' wisdom and loyalty required references to Scripture by both Satan and God. Satan concealed his reliance on self-interest behind persuasive citations from the law. His seductions could be penetrated only by God's disclosure of a true reading purged of self-interest and consequent deception. The inner linkage between Satan's deceptions and human thinking came to the surface in Jesus' rebuke of Peter when Peter protested that suffering surely could not be the fate of the Messiah. A similar linkage may be discerned behind the standard interpretations of Scripture offered by the scribes and lawyers. Like Peter, they had succumbed to Satan's wiles. This fact emerges when one compares the logic of Satan's initial temptation ("If you are the Son of God") and the logic of the final taunt of Jesus' enemies ("If he were the Son of God he would save himself and come down from the cross").

The authors of the Gospels were also keenly aware of the bearing that Jesus' struggles with Satan had on the later inner struggles of Jesus' followers. Like him, they confronted professional interpreters of the Scripture who were adept in disproving Christian claims about the Messiah. Satan was always ready to exploit their desires to escape the martyrdom that loyalty to Jesus might entail. The accounts of Jesus' testing must have seemed to them like the original etchings of which their own testings were copies. The problem they faced was not the intellectual problem of how to interpret an ancient myth. Rather, each of them was engaged in a vocation for which the stakes were all or nothing, especially when they, like him, were forced to cry, "Why have you forsaken me?"

Nor should we overlook later periods of Christian history, such as the time when the church was making its choices of documents that should be accepted as inspired and therefore authoritative. In those choices, one of the considerations that weighed heavily was whether the Father and the Son continued to speak to the church through a given document. During that long period, how did churches respond in worship to these conversations in which Satan disclosed his deceptive power most persuasively and in which God disclosed an opposing ability to unmask his archetypal enemy? Such stories exerted a recurring power to remind Christians that the same conflicts were lurking within their hearts and that victories in those conflicts required a quiet reliance on the presence of the Risen Lord, who was still able to keep them from falling. It took only a whiff of danger, then as now, to remind Christ's followers of the definitions that the Messiah had given to the father/son/family metaphor. The usual definitions were those in which human beings accepted Satan's language; the true definitions were those in which a single person had once and for all disclosed God's language. Understood in these terms, the Gospel stories of conflicts between God and Satan reveal two opposing linguistic systems. Such stories are few in number, but they are rightly located at the beginning, the middle, and the end of the Gospels, or better, at the decisive points in the struggle between the Divine and the demonic. That cosmic struggle furnished the ultimate horizons for decisions made in the heart. Those decisions, in turn, furnished a pinpoint focus for the universal drama.

THE EVANGELISTS
AND
GOD

THE EVANGELISTS
AND
GOD

"He has put down the mighty from their thrones" (Luke 1:51).
That statement does not spring from harmless wordplay
with hyperbole. It announces God's successful attack
upon all forms of power.

The three documents that have served as a literary basis for this study (Mark, Matthew, and Luke) are the work of three authors who were alike in that all three were Christians writing for members of Christian churches. The authors and their readers were bound together by loyalty to the God who had disclosed himself to them as the Father of their Lord Jesus Christ. The authors and some of their readers were charismatic leaders of churches, recipients of the Holy Spirit as apostles, prophets, and teachers. As successors to Jesus' original disciples, they found a direct vocational relevance in the texts surveyed in section 1 of this study. Engaged in more or less open conflict with adversaries who were to some degree successors of Jesus' adversaries, they found guidance and support in the texts surveyed in section 2. They had also undergone inner struggles endemic to their vocation, struggles between God and Satan over interpretations of Scripture and over the costs of fidelity to a martyred Messiah (see the texts in sect. 3). Considering their personal involvement in the traditions they edited, it is remarkable that they concealed themselves so completely within those traditions. Only occasionally, and then only by conjecture, can a modern reader detect their fingerprints as editors.

Covert signs of their work may take different forms. In some cases, they interjected into the narrative a Scripture citation that represented their own understanding of what had happened. In other cases, they found that a hymn that had become current in their churches expressed the inner meaning of events that had been hidden from the original participants. In still other cases, they reported the message of an angel to one of the human participants or the message of a prophet that conveyed an inspiration by the Holy Spirit. Behind such editorial comments lie several assumptions. For one thing, the stories are based on the conviction that the will and hand of God had been active in what had happened. With divine foresight, God had seen the end from the beginning, so that stories of such beginnings could now be retold in the light of that end, which to each Evangelist now lay in the past. Often, in telling the story, the narrator made it clear that the human participants had not been able to anticipate this later harvest of an earlier planting. But readers of the Gospels were in a more privileged position. They themselves represented that harvest. They accepted, as natural literary conventions, the narrators' accounts of visits made by angels, dream-visions of key individuals, utterances of prophets, allusions to Scripture and to familiar hymns.

As a result, the stories fused the external happenings, accessible to human view, with the inner meanings that had become revealed only lately.

Because this is the character of these stories, their interpretation confronts modern readers with many problems. Where should the line be drawn between visible happenings and invisible meanings? Is it legitimate to use ancient prophecies, for example, from Isaiah, to explain the birth of Jesus, when Isaiah could not have had Jesus in mind? Must one share Matthew's doctrine of angels to accept his symbolic story of the flight into Egypt? In oral traditions that had taken their shape in the pre-Gospel period, is it valid to attribute their shape to the Evangelist, who was the final editor? None of these problems can be solved easily.

We may avoid some of them, however, for our concern here is limited to two questions. What inferences can safely be drawn from each text regarding the Evangelists' attitude toward God? For our purpose it is sufficient to suppose that, because an Evangelist chose such a story, it reflects to some degree his own basic outlook. What linkage can be discerned between a given text and the testimonies to God that have been found in the texts reviewed in sections 1–3? The greater the number of such linkages, the more we can be assured that the basic attitudes of the Evangelists are being brought to the surface. Focusing on those two questions may prove useful. In addition, they may corroborate the results of study in the earlier sections.

TEXTS

77. On Turning Hearts

78. The Given Name

79. Israel's Ruler

80. Two Impossible Children

81. The Heart's Imagination

82. A Prophet's Doxology

83. The Angel's Anthem

84. An Old Man's Vision

85. A Logger's Ax

86. The Incredible News

87. God Chooses a Servant

88. God Arouses Fear

89. God Speaks Through Vision

90. To Be Continued

    Retrospect

77   On Turning Hearts

TEXT

The angel to Zechariah, about John:
> And he will turn many of the sons of Israel to the Lord their God,
> and he will go before him in the spirit and power of Elijah,
> to turn the hearts of the fathers to the children,
> and the disobedient to the wisdom of the just,
> to make ready for the Lord a people prepared. (Luke 1:16–17)

SITUATION

Luke 1:8–25

The angel Gabriel, standing in the presence of God, announces to Zechariah the results of John's work. This message is an answer to a priest's prayer in the temple.

INFERENCES

God is the true Lord of the sons of Israel.

God is to become known to Israel through the work of the prophet John.

God will thus fulfill promises made in and through Elijah.

God seeks to reconcile alienated groups within Israel—the disobedient and the just, the fathers and the sons.

All this is good news from God, relayed through Gabriel and through John to penitent Israelites and finally to Luke's readers.

LINKAGES

In other texts Jesus and his disciples are also sent to Israel.

Zechariah's doubts (vs. 18) anticipate similar reactions, on the part of sons of Israel and priests, to later messages of Jesus and his messengers.

John prepares a people only by turning hearts, by winning over the disobedient through the work of prophets.

This text, like others, recognizes divisions within Israel and God's determination to overcome them.

God's answers to Zechariah's prayers express Luke's faith in God's power to answer many other prayers for the equally incredible and impossible.

ON COMPARING THE BIRTH STORIES

Childs, *The New Testament as Canon: An Introduction* (Philadelphia: Fortress Press, 1985), pp. 158–65.

78 The Given Name

TEXT All this took place to fulfill what the Lord [God] had spoken by the prophet [Isaiah]:
"Think of it! A virgin will conceive and bear a son.
His name will be called Emmanuel (that is, God with us)."

(Matt. 1:22–23)

SITUATION Matthew 1:18–25; Isaiah 7:14; 8:8; Luke 1:31
Matthew, the Evangelist, comments on the angel's message to Joseph.
In the chain of revelation are God, Isaiah, angel, Joseph, Matthew, readers.

INFERENCES In Jesus, God has come to be with "us."
God's presence in Jesus is the fulfillment of prophecy.
Looking back from this fulfillment, we can see connections between Isaiah, Joseph, the Virgin, Jesus, ourselves, the future.
Being "God with us," Jesus speaks to us with the authority of God.
Jesus' name expresses God's presence, power, authority, life.
It is only through Jesus that God chooses whom to be with.
The "us" includes the whole chain of prophets and generations, a miraculous, mysterious time- and space-spanning community.
The witness of God includes the salvation of his people from their sins (Matt. 1:21).

LINKAGES The stories that tell of God's choice of Jesus' names (Jesus, Emmanuel) include references to God, Isaiah, the angel, Mary, Joseph, sins, salvation, visions, dreams, shame, fear, human obedience.
The Evangelist retrojects this syndrome of significant Christian language into the birth story as a whole.
The birth story, so interpreted, anticipates the climax of the story in the death and resurrection. There, too, Jesus is equivalent to "God with us" (Matt. 28:20).
Every example of being-with-Jesus is a point of being-with-God, of earth meeting heaven.
This witness indicates the importance of all the commands of Jesus, inasmuch as they become commands of God.

GOD WITH US—IN PRISON dePury, *Journal from My Cell*, pp. 50–57.

79   Israel's Ruler

TEXT
So it is written in the prophet:
"You, O Bethlehem, in the land of Judah,
    are by no means least among the rulers of Judah,
    for from you shall come a ruler
    who will shepherd my people Israel." (Matt. 2:5–6)

SITUATION
Matthew 2:1–12; Micah 5:2 (cf. Luke 1:26–38)
Matthew's comment on the answer of the chief priests and scribes to Herod
"My people" means God's people; God is speaking through the prophet.
"A ruler" means Jesus, coming from Bethlehem. Note the irony, in view of
    the later history, that these words are said in the presence of the priests,
    scribes, and Herod.

INFERENCES
God is the one who spoke through Micah and who now fulfills that prophecy.
God continues to exert his authority to anoint kings of Israel.
God's anointed ruler will replace Herod and earthly kingdoms, but the
    unending character of God's kingdom distinguishes it sharply from
    earthly analogues.
In fulfilling his plan, God speaks through priests, scribes, visiting kings, and
    Herod, even though they do not understand their roles.
God's plan succeeds in spite of all efforts by Israel's kings and priests to
    thwart it (cf. John 11:50).

LINKAGES
The basic contrasts between Herod's language and Matthew's is illustrated by
    the double meanings of the terms prophet, priest, king, Israel.
This Word of God enables the church to claim its continuity with Israel in
    spite of the hostility of priests and kings.
The church's language about Israel and its rulers has a timeless reference (he
    will govern forever) in contrast to the time-bound reference to the
    priests, the scribes, and the king.
The metaphor of kingship dominates the Passion story no less than it does the
    birth story.
Changes in all ideas of king as applied to the Risen Jesus produce
    corresponding changes in all ideas of God as king.
God's kingdom is to other kingdoms as he is to the other kings.

ON CELEBRATING CHRISTMAS
Lilje, *Valley of the Shadow*, pp. 80–85.

80   Two Impossible Children

TEXT   Mary: How can this be, since I have no husband?
Gabriel: The Holy Spirit will come upon you,
    and the power of the Most High will overshadow you;
    therefore the child to be born will be called holy,
    the son of God.
Listen! Your kinswoman Elizabeth in her old age has also conceived a son. . . .
For with God nothing will be impossible! (Luke 1:34–37)

SITUATION   Luke 1:26–38
The annunciation to Mary concerning the births of John and Jesus

INFERENCES   The power of God and the power of the Holy Spirit are responsible for the two
    births.
Every authentic promise of God (vs. 37) carries with it the power of
    actualization.
In accordance with this promise, other sons will also be born.
The fulfillment of God's other promises to Israel is no less possible.
The contrast between what is impossible for human beings and what is possible
    for God underlies the whole Gospel story.
Holiness is to be recognized in what God does through his chosen sons.

LINKAGES   To other texts in which the actions of the Holy Spirit are expressions of God's
    purpose and power
To other texts that explain incredible events in terms of God's purpose and
    presence
To the texts that trace to God the revelation of who his Son is
To texts in which the advent of the kingdom appears among the lowliest people
    and in the most surprising places

**WHAT KIND
OF HISTORY IS THIS?**   Paul S. Minear, "The Interpreter and the Nativity Stories," *Theology Today*
7(1950–51): 358–75.

81   The Heart's Imagination

TEXT
    Elizabeth (or Mary):
        My spirit rejoices in God my savior,
        for he has looked upon the humiliation of his slave. . . .
        His mercy is on those who fear him
            from generation to generation. . . .
        He has scattered the proud in the imagination of
            their hearts,
        He has put down the mighty from their thrones,
        And has exalted the humble. (Luke 1:47–48, 50–52)

SITUATION
    Luke 1:45–55; 1 Samuel 2:1–10
    Poem, song, prophecy—covering the entire action of God
    The response of Elizabeth or Mary to the births of John and Jesus
    The celebration of salvation, in prospect and retrospect, by individual ("my")
        and church ("our")

INFERENCES
    God's salvation of Israel embraces not only one woman but, through her, all
        generations.
    God's action turns human positions of weakness, slavery, humiliation,
        poverty, and emptiness upside down.
    This action is done within hearts, without altering social position or economic
        security.
    It is the unexpected mercy of God that works this heart-miracle and releases
        joy, fear, and blessedness.

LINKAGES
    Like the story, this song is composed of bits of many Scripture prophecies
        that were used in early Christian worship.
    Mary and Elizabeth speak for lowly and repentant Israel as God's chosen
        people from all generations.
    The two mothers are presented as typical of discipleship.
    The "proud" are typical of later Lukan pictures of Jesus' adversaries.
    The song is a demonstration of the truth of Luke 1:37.
    The many similarities to the song of Hannah (1 Sam. 2:1–10) indicate
        common traditions of how to celebrate the birth of a prophet.
    Many allusions to the Old Testament can be detected in this hymn. (1 Sam.
        1:11; Job 5:11; 12:19; Isa. 41:8; Ps. 89:10; 98:3; 103:17; 107:9; 111:9).

A COMPOSER ALSO SINGS
    Johann Sebastian Bach, *Magnificat,* S. 243, D Major.

82   A Prophet's Doxology

TEXT   Zechariah:
>   Blessed be the Lord God of Israel
>   for he has visited and redeemed his people,
>   and has raised up a horn of salvation for us
>   in the house of his servant David. . . .
>   to give light to those who sit in darkness and in the shadow of death,
>   to guide our feet into the way of peace. (Luke 1:68–69, 79)

SITUATION   Luke 1:68–79
Poem, song, prophecy of what God has done and will do through John and Jesus
Constructed out of Scripture and reminiscences of the work of Jesus
Liturgical use

INFERENCES   The knowledge of God is a knowledge of forgiveness of sins.
This knowledge is correlated with the way of peace, with light in darkness, with life for the dying, with deliverance from enemies.
God pledged and has kept his pledge to the patriarchs.
God's mercy produces holiness and righteousness.
John's preparation for Jesus fulfills God's plan.
Jesus, coming from the house of David, has fulfilled God's covenant with Abraham.
The song is wholly consonant with the later work of John and Jesus as prophetic revealers of God's salvation.

LINKAGES   The picture of "our enemies" fits pictures of later conflict.
The poem/song/prophecy is typical of the work of early Christian prophets (note especially "he has").
The song suggests that God's action is best expressed in doxologies such as this.
As in many other texts, God is known through his promises to the patriarchs and through the work of such prophets as John and Jesus and their successors.
As in many other texts, the heart is the scene of God's miracles; the gratitude is inward, subjective, communal, Spirit-guided. Recognition of his mercy creates a boundary between us and our enemies.

SONGS OF OTHER PROPHETS   Odes of Solomon 7—14

83   The Angel's Anthem

TEXT A multitude of the heavenly host, praising God and singing:
"Glory to God in the highest,
And on earth peace among those with whom he is pleased!" (Luke 2:13–14)

SITUATION Luke 2:1–14; 19:38; Psalm 118:26
The visit of the angels to the Bethlehem shepherds
A greeting to Jesus on his arrival in Jerusalem
A liturgical doxology

INFERENCES The glory of God and the peace of his people are viewed as inseparable.
The people's worship and the angels' song are inseparable.
Both are invisible. God is worshiped where there is no audible worship; his
  peace is celebrated on earth, where no peace is available.
The doxology of the angels leads to the doxologies of the shepherds (Luke
  2:20), who, in caring for their flocks, are symbols of later shepherds.
The occasion for glorifying God means good news of great joy (v. 10).
  Anthems in heaven express the joy on earth.

LINKAGES To other texts dealing with peace as God's gift to his people
To other texts expressing the joy of God's slaves
To the linguistic world in which the glory of God, shared by the people as
  God's elect, constitutes the infrastructure of reality
To the idea of peacemakers as sons of God
To God's joy over the repentance of sinners
To other references to angels, where we find angels filling the same double
  role: praising God and conferring peace on earth

MIRACLE OR HISTORY Karl Barth, *Epistle to the Romans*, ch. 3, comment on Romans 3:22b–24.

84 An Old Man's Vision

TEXT

Simeon . . . blessed God and sang:
Lord, now let your servant depart in peace . . .
for I have seen your salvation,
which you have prepared in the presence of all peoples,
a light for revelation to the Gentiles
and for glory to your people Israel. (Luke 2:28–32)

SITUATION

Luke 2:22–35
In the temple Simeon, a prophet inspired by the Holy Spirit, utters a prayer of
thanksgiving for God's gift of salvation in Jesus.

INFERENCES

God's salvation is universal in intention and scope. It operates as a light to
Gentiles and brings glory to Israel.
God fulfills his promise to such individual prophets as Simeon (vs. 26; cf. Mark
9:1).
Such fulfillment is a way by which God reveals the thoughts of many hearts
(vs. 35).
It is also a way by which God has produced bitter divisions within Israel and
Jesus' own family (vs. 34).
The prophet's song is appropriate as a summary of what God has done through
Jesus.
Luke assumes that the singing of such a song is appropriately assigned to the
temple.

LINKAGES

To other texts that announce God's gift to Israel
To the announcement of the inclusion both of Gentiles and of Jews in God's
kingdom
To assurances of the fulfillment of the law (vs. 22), the temple (vs. 27), earlier
prophecies and God's Word (vs. 29), and the coming of the Holy Spirit
To other prophecies that Jesus' ministry would produce conflicts within Israel,
both before and after Jesus' death
To the repertoire of early Christian hymns and benedictions, many of which are
centered in the act of blessing and glorifying God

A SUMMARY

John Calvin, *Institutes of the Christian Religion*, vol. 2, aphorisms 1–13.

85   A Logger's Ax

TEXT

Luke: All flesh shall see the salvation of God.
John: Who warned you to flee from the wrath to come? . . .
Do not begin to say to yourselves, "We have Abraham as our father"; for I tell you, God is able from these stones to raise up children to Abraham. Even now the axe is laid to the root of the trees. (Luke 3:6–9)

SITUATION

Luke 3:1–14; Matthew 3:1–10; Luke 7:24–35; Matthew 11:7–19; Isaiah 40:3–5
Isaiah's prophecy pointing to John; John's prophecy pointing to Jesus
Sequence of prophecies in Luke: Mary, Zechariah, Simeon, Anna, John
John's announcement of judgment, baptism, and forgiveness in Jesus

INFERENCES

God authorized this call for repentance for the forgiveness of sins.
It was God who warned the brood of vipers to flee the coming wrath.
Sonship to Abraham offered no immunity to God's judgment.
God could (and did) create Abraham's children from stones (sinners, tax
    collectors, lepers, Gentiles).
Because repentance is an act of total disarmament, no easier for individuals
    than for nations, it is an act that signals God's power to level mountains
    (Luke 3:5).

LINKAGES

To prophecies linking final judgment to repentance
To the elimination of all privileges for the righteous
To attacks on the self-deceptions encouraged by the membership and the
    leadership in Israel
To salvation defined as forgiveness of sins and as a way by which the last
    becomes first

ABRAHAM AND HIS SON

Søren Kierkegaard, *Fear and Trembling*, trans. Walter Lowrie (Princeton: Princeton University Press, 1941), pp. 17–30.

86 The Incredible News

TEXT Now after John was arrested, Jesus came into Galilee, preaching the good news of God and saying, "The time is fulfilled, and the kingdom of God is at hand. Repent and believe in the good news." (Mark 1:14–15)

SITUATION Mark 1:14–15; Matthew 4:12–17
Jesus' opening message; for Mark the epitome of the good news

INFERENCES The reference to John indicates continuity between the work of the two prophets, both of whom speak on God's authority (Mark 11:27–33).
The reference to John's arrest implies the risk of arrest for Jesus.
God's news has to do with the approach and the accessibility of his kingdom.
But this news can only be accepted on faith, because there is no evidence for it apart from the prophet's word.
Faith takes the form of repentance as the sole requirement.
Such repentance requires movement of the heart from saying "God's kingdom cannot possibly be here" to saying "the time is fulfilled."

LINKAGES The delivery of this news fuses three twin images: father/son, sender/sent, king/kingdom.
What the act of repentance covers is suggested by many other terms: solidarity with the least, last, meek, humble, lowly, poor, hungry, paralyzed, captives, lost sheep.
Other texts that present the kingdom as final judgment are here linked to texts in which the kingdom is accessible in the present as God's gift to the helpless and hopeless.
This text is followed immediately by the call of four disciples, indicating that this news is the message they, too, will be authorized to proclaim.

ON AVOIDING REPENTANCE Francis Thompson, "The Hound of Heaven," in *Poems and Essays*, ed. Wilfred Meynell, 3 vols. in one (Freeport, N.Y.: Books for Libraries Press, 1969), vol. 1, pp. 107–113.

87   God Chooses a Servant

TEXT

This was to fulfill what was spoken by the prophet Isaiah:
"Look! Here is my servant whom I have chosen,
    my beloved with whom I am well pleased.
I will put my Spirit upon him,
    and he will proclaim justice to the Gentiles. . . .
    and in his name the Gentiles will hope." (Matt. 12:17–18)

SITUATION

Matthew 12:1–21; Isaiah 42:1–4
"I" refers to God; "my servant" refers to Jesus.
The Evangelist comments on Jesus' response to the Pharisees' hostility and
    on his success in healing on the sabbath.

INFERENCES

Isaiah's word is taken as referring both to God's choice of Jesus ("I have
    chosen") and to God's future action ("the Gentiles will hope").
God approves of Jesus' gentleness against the violence of his enemies and his
    respect for the vulnerability of the helpless.
God's Spirit is present in the proclamation to the Gentiles, even though no
    voice is heard in the streets.
Jesus' death is seen as a way by which God "brings justice to victory."
    Strange justice this.
God's justice requires both the success of the plot against Jesus (Matt. 12:14)
    and the quiet, nonviolent behavior of God's servant (vss. 19–20).

LINKAGES

This is one of Matthew's summaries of the whole mission of Jesus and of
    God's authorization and presence in that mission.
The paradox of proclamation by silence is typical of God's action in the
    Gospels.
The gift of the Holy Spirit is seen to be essential to the mission; it links God's
    work in Jesus to his work in the disciples.
The gentleness of Jesus (and God) is linked here to Jesus' (and God's) power
    to heal paralysis, blindness, dumbness.
Every work of God to heal Gentiles or Jews is subject to a double
    interpretation: i.e., God or Beelzebul?
Matthew sees Jesus' work in the synagogue (12:9) as continued in his
    proclamation to the Gentiles (vs. 18), though the latter work began only
    after Jesus' death.

ON SINGING THEOLOGY

Martin Luther, "A Mighty Fortress Is Our God" (hymn)

88 God Arouses Fear

TEXT
Fear seized them all: and they glorified God, saying, "A great prophet has arisen among us!" and "God has visited his people!" (Luke 7:16)

SITUATION
Luke 7:11–17
The Evangelist comments upon the reaction of the disciples and the crowds to Jesus' raising of a widow's only son and his restoration of the son to his mother (Israel?).
The miracle and the reaction are taken as typical.

INFERENCES
The appearance of a prophet means a visit by God to his people.
What this prophet has said and done is a sign of that visit.
Approval of the prophet's action calls for observers to glorify God.
This one cure is representative of many.
All the healings are linked to proclamations of good news to the poor; i.e., announcing God's blessing on the various kinds of desperate human needs that people are themselves helpless to alleviate.
The presence of God in these actions arouses fear (vs. 16).
The same presence provokes many to take offense (to be caused to stumble) at Jesus' work.

LINKAGES
Raising the dead calls to mind other texts, illustrating both radical change in a person's condition and a correction of the usual definitions of death.
Other stories of Jesus' healing indicate fear as a typical response.
In the midcourse of Jesus' ministry, this comment by Luke recalls his opening keynote (4:16–30).
Like other texts, this story finds God at work, not in cosmic catastrophes, plagues, economic conditions, or the history of nations, but in help offered to individuals in need.
The glorification of God is the natural response to specific visits to specific individuals.

THOUGHTS ON MIRACLES
Joachim Jeremias, *New Testament Theology*, trans. John Bowden (New York: Charles Scribner's Sons, 1971), pp. 86–96.

89 God Speaks Through Vision

TEXT A cloud overshadowed them, and a voice came out of the cloud: "This is my beloved Son; listen to him." (Mark 9:7)

SITUATION Mark 9:2–13; Matthew 17:1–8; Luke 9:28–36

The mountain of transfiguration, where three disciples see a vision of Moses, Elijah, and Jesus, and hear these words from God

The scene is located immediately after the prediction of the coming death and before the start of the journey to Jerusalem.

The incident was not reported until after the resurrection.

INFERENCES God reveals to three key apostles his approval of Jesus as his beloved Son.

God gives his seal to the continuity between Moses (the law), Elijah (the prophets), and Jesus, as fulfillment of the earlier history of Israel.

The scene preserves the mystery of God's presence while authorizing Jesus to speak for God; it makes obedience to Jesus an essential form of obedience to God.

The vision gives the apostles the authority to speak for Jesus and for God.

The vision assumes that the real, heavenly world is hidden from human sight and hearing, except when God takes the initiative in identifying his messengers.

The disciples misunderstand the vision and the voice.

Mark relates their current misunderstanding to their misunderstanding of Jesus' suffering (Mark 9:12).

LINKAGES This "Listen" is the only command in the Gospels attributed to God himself. As such, it can be interpreted as covering all situations, all periods of time, all disciples, all proclamations of the gospel.

The scene is a disclosure, not to Jesus, but to apostles. It takes a literary form of a prophetic call: the opened heaven, a vision, a voice, a command, a commission, a prediction of future activity involving suffering. Its basic function is the qualification of leaders for later assignments (cf. all texts in sect. 1).

VISION AND REALITY Terrien, *Elusive Presence*, pp. 422–28.

90 To Be Continued

TEXT An angel to grieving women:
> Go, tell his disciples and Peter that he is going before you to Galilee. You will see him there, as he told you. (Mark 16:7)

SITUATION Mark 16:1–8; Matthew 28:1–10; Mark 14:26–28
The tomb of Jesus on the first day of the week
Instructions issued by an angel, presumably from God, intended for Jesus' disciples

INFERENCES This message is from God, who has guided the whole story of Jesus from the beginning.
The instructions make clear God's concern that Jesus' assignment should be continued by the disciples.
Visions of the Risen Jesus constitute a necessary step in that transfer of authority.
Such visions produce amazement and fear, even speechlessness, but the work will go on.

LINKAGES To the other accounts of the exaltation of Jesus and the gift of the Spirit
To earlier accounts of the call and commissioning of the disciples
To texts that trace the authority of the disciples to its heavenly source
To other illustrations of the belief that words from God have been entrusted for delivery by men and women

RESURRECTION AS VOCATION Rowan Williams, *Resurrection: Interpreting the Easter Gospel* (New York: Pilgrim Press, 1984), pp. 86–97.

RETROSPECT

In his provocative book *The Nature of Doctrine*, George A. Lindbeck has offered in a single sentence both a description of what Scripture does and a prescription for what interpretation should do. "Scripture," he wrote, "creates its own domain of meaning," and interpreters are obliged "to extend this over the whole of reality" (p. 117). In dealing with three segments of Scripture, the Synoptic Gospels, we have attempted to explore this domain of meaning insofar as it is centered in patterns of thinking about God. The authors of those Gospels were themselves among the earliest interpreters of that domain of meaning, and it is clear that they believed that it extended over the whole of reality.

In their work they developed what Leander Keck has called "a grammar of correlations," in which thinking about God is fused with thinking about other things in such a way as to illuminate both correlatives. As a way of concluding this study, then, I will itemize some of those correlations.

To begin, it is clear that the Evangelists discerned very close linkage between thinking about God and the story of Jesus Christ. The whole story of the Son is a disclosure of the will and ways of the Father. In fact, that is the meaning of his being sent. As Jon Sobrino wrote, "Jesus' life makes sense only in terms of his awareness of this mission" (*Christology at the Crossroads*, p. 72).

Jesus' mission entailed the creation of a wider family of brothers, sisters, mothers—all becoming children of God by way of acts of humility and obedience, babes whose purity of heart enabled them to forgive their debtors and to love their enemies. Members of this family found that their thinking about God was closely correlated with participation in his creation of this new family.

However, they recognized that God had sent the Messiah to Israel, that in the Messiah, God had fulfilled promises made to the patriarchs, had continued the line of prophets and seers (from Abel, through Moses, Elijah, Elisha, Zechariah), and that even the inclusion of Gentiles within the family had been a fulfillment of God's designs already disclosed in the call of Abraham. The Evangelists did not destroy but confirmed the correlation between thinking about God and thinking about God's elect people.

The realism of this correlation was indicated by an awareness of the age-old recalcitrance of Israel. The chain of God's messengers to Israel had provoked a chain of rejections by Israel; the cross of the Messiah was itself a culmination of this history of crucifixions. The Gospel writers extended this domain of meaning to cover not only the history of the chosen people but also the total history of Adam's descendants.

It is not surprising, then, that their grammar included a correlation of thinking about God with thinking about his age-long conflict with Satan, a warfare involving both heaven and earth but centering on earth in Israel's rebellion against God. Indeed, this rebellion continued in the self-willed fears and infidelities of the followers of the Messiah. It was reflection on this wider struggle that placed in proper perspective the more immediate issues of choosing God or mammon, God or Caesar.

The grammar of correlations gave a central place to the linkage between the Father's will and what transpired in the hearts of his children. He knew them better than they knew themselves. He detected sins of which they were entirely unaware. Before a word could appear on their lips, he was at work in their souls. What they prized, he detested. Because he created the inside as well as the outside, it was from within that all desires emerged, reflecting an origin in either the will of Satan or the will of God.

Of course God was recognized as both primal creator and final judge; but it was his activity in the present that disclosed the meanings of ultimate beginnings and endings. The parables of future judgment were little more than parables of what really happens when God invades the familiar world with devastating threats and miraculous promises. It was in the act of repentance that the Evangelists discovered the relevance of both threat and promise.

It is clear that the new family discerned clear correlations between the law and the prophets and the actions of the Father. The interpretation of the new domain of meaning required an extensive pattern of ideas about Scripture. In fact, it was in divergent conceptions of Scripture that the battle line formed between Jesus and his adversaries. At great risk of oversimplifying I suggest that for Christ's new family the axis between God and the heart became the primary location of God's new creation. Existing before the law, this activity enabled this family to discern God's original purposes in the law (e.g. God created the sabbath for human beings). In contrast, the lawyers gave priority to God's creation of the law and insisted that God's relation to the heart be regulated by the law as a prior creation.

Many other correlations might be suggested, but these may be sufficient to indicate that the new patterns of thinking about God were elements in a new life-world and thought-world in which all key words received new connotations. (Examples of this new vocabulary have been given in earlier pages, so there is no need for repetition here.)

However, let me make a final plea that you recognize how fundamental and how shattering such a conversion in familiar words can be. For instance, consider a strange story from the book of Acts. It is a tale of how the Jewish leaders in Thessalonica incited a mob to shout, "These men [the apostles] who have turned the world upside down have come here as well" (Acts 17:6). Such a shout seems curious when we realize that these Apostles had not demanded any change in the form of government, in the economic system, or in the existing echelons of prestige and power. Why, then, the charge of upending the world? They were turning the familiar world upside down simply by turning its language upside down. When wealth becomes poverty, and humiliation glory, and death life—when such things happen, nothing can ever again be the same. The human habitat is a world created by its language; a new language and a new creation come into existence at the same moment. And only a community's Deity has enough power to serve as such a creator.

One further observation may be added concerning the implications of the texts reviewed in this last section. I make this comment in answer to a simple question: in what specific context in the life of early Christians does this grammar of correlations fit most naturally? Considering the number of hymns and chants, doxologies and benedictions, citations from Scripture and prophetic declamations, only one answer seems cogent. The grammar of correlations is nothing but the grammar native to Christian worship, as the family of God's children assemble for prayer and praise, for baptism and the eucharist, for listening to the Word and sharing in the gifts of the Spirit. Seen in this light, the Gospels become examples of liturgical theology, and we must view their authors as liturgical theologians.

These texts place the center of gravity for theological reflection, not in speaking of God's role in the origins of the cosmos or of God's control of international conflict, but in articulating his immediate and continuing activity within a particular community to whom he has given particular promises. "He has visited and redeemed his people." He has fulfilled those promises through a chain of specific individuals whose vocation has consisted of mediating his presence and his will to this people. "Here is my servant whom I have chosen." The fulfillment of those promises, as in "turning the hearts of the fathers to the children," enabled worshipers to sense the continuing presence of earlier generations. The fulfillment of other promises, in turn, such as "the kingdom of God is at hand," established their fellowship with coming generations. The texts also telescoped the distance between heaven and earth. Moved by the Spirit, congregations could sing with Simeon, "My eyes have seen your salvation." Working shepherds could hear the angels' anthems without difficulty. Prayer brought the will of God within the reach of earth, "as it is done in heaven." The kingdom of God, now identified with the kingdom of Christ, ceased to be a hypothetical possibility for some later time and some other place; it became tangibly present in the communal celebration of God's power and glory. Although that kingdom had no end, it had very definite beginnings among those who repented their earlier blindness to its coming. Although such beginnings elicited canticles that expressed the ecstasies of the saved, they also conveyed warnings of a coming time of troubles. Every baptism was followed by a time of testing. Each true prophecy announced "a rising and a falling of many in Israel." A sword would pierce a mother's heart; Herod would massacre many innocent children of Rachel; trusted leaders would be deceived and would betray the faith. At the eucharist, Jesus continued to feed disciples who neither understood his mission nor were prepared to pay its cost. Thus the Evangelists preserved the realism of God's good news.

Even so, Christians at worship rejoiced in the reconciliation of age-long enmities between Jews and Gentiles: "revelation to the Gentiles . . . and glory to your people Israel." The greater the hostility from both groups, the greater the miracle when Jews and Gentiles were able to worship together through the power of the Holy Spirit. The texts also reflect a new unity between men and women in worship. Angels visited both Mary and Joseph. Miracles were wrought on Zechariah and Elizabeth. In the temple Anna joined Simeon in prophetic witness. The birth stories also rightly reflect the fact that Christian worship took place in an aura of mystery and miracle. A similar aura surrounded the stories of resurrection and rebirth. It was not the realm of magic, as if one earthly empire were suddenly replaced by another or as if an economy of hunger were suddenly transformed into an economy of plenty. Rather, the message of God's victory over Satan opened hearts to "a new heaven and a new earth," a habitat where stories of the blind receiving sight became quite natural and necessary symbols of revelation. In such a habitat, liturgical theology became doxological theology; it found in "psalms and hymns and spiritual songs" a most subtle and imaginative form of thinking about God. It is by no means strange that the Magnificat and the Benedictus, the Nunc Dimittis and the Gloria, have become regular features in the musical repertoire of the church. These lines in the Gospels almost certainly originated in the worship of the church during the period before the three Evangelists edited the traditions used in that worship.

But the worship contained more than music. Those who sang of peace on earth were potential martyrs, summoned to the mount of transfiguration to hear the voice out of the cloud, "This is my son. Listen to him." That was the Word that each worshiping congregation was commanded to hear and to obey.

INDICES

Index of Scripture Texts

Mark	Text
1:1–11	67
1:14–15	86
1:35–38	1
2:1–12	48
2:23–28	49
3:6	48
3:22–27	47
3:31–35	6
6:35, 36	22
7:1–23	50
8:27–33	5
8:31–33	23, 71
8:34–38	36
9:1	36
9:2–13	89
9:37	3
10:1–12	63
10:17–22	44
10:23–31	37
10:35–45	67
11:15–19	46
11:25	21
11:27–33	86
11:30	67
12:1–12	58
12:13–17	60
12:18–27	61, 62
12:26–27	62
12:28–34	45
12:35–37	59
13:9–13	9
13:14–20	33
13:30–37	34, 73
14:26–28	40, 90
14:32–42	73
14:55–65	65
15:22–32	66
15:22–37	74
16:1–8	90

Luke	Text
1:8–25	77
1:26–38	80
1:31	78
1:37	37
1:45–55	81
1:68–79	82
2:1–14	83
2:22–35	84
3:1–14	85
3:21, 22	67
4:1–4	76
4:1–13	76
4:5–8	70
4:9–12	69
4:16–30	43, 76, 88
4:42, 43	1
5:17–26	48

(Luke)	Text
5:19–29	61
6:1–5	49
6:35–36	22
7:11–17	88
7:24–30	2
7:29, 30	57
7:24–35	85
8:19–21	16
9:18–22	5, 71
9:23–27	36
9:28–36	89
9:48	3
10:1, 2	38
10:1–18	12
10:16	3
10:17–24	4, 72
10:19, 20	13
10:25–28	45
11:2–4	26
11:9–13	14
11:14–23	47
11:27, 28	7
11:37–41	52
11:42–44	53
11:45–51	64
12:4–7	10
12:4–9	8
12:6, 7	11
12:9	36
12:13–21	35
12:22–31	14
12:50	67
14:16–24	56
15:1–32	55
15:3–7	29
16:13–15	54
18:1–8	32
18:9–14	31
18:18–30	44
18:24–30	37
19:38	83
19:45–48	46
20:9–19	58
20:20–26	60
20:27–40	61, 62
20:38	62
20:41–44	59
21:12–19	9
21:32–36	34
22:28–30	27
22:40–46	73
22:66–71	65
23:2	60
23:26–34	75
23:33–38	66
23:44–46	76
23:44–49	41

John	Text
1:1–18	7
2:13–17	46
5:19–29	62
12:27–33	26, 73
12:44, 45	3
13:20	3
14:27	39
15:14	6
19:15	60

Acts	
1:6–8	34, 41, 76
1:22	67
2	37, 76
2:16–21	41
7:51–60	76
7:55–60	25
10:36–38	67

Romans	
3:9–20	44
14:7–9	62

1 Corinthians	
1:26–31	72
7:10–11	63
10:31	26

2 Corinthians	
1:17–20	24

Philippians	
1:27—2:13	9

Hebrews	
2:13	6
10:1–10	53, 73
12:14, 22–24	25, 39

James	
5:12	24

1 Peter	
1:23–25	7
3:1–12	63

Revelation	
4—5	26

Index of Authors and Titles